797,885 Books
are available to read at

Forgotten Books

www.ForgottenBooks.com

Forgotten Books' App
Available for mobile, tablet & eReader

ISBN 978-1-330-05179-5
PIBN 10013676

This book is a reproduction of an important historical work. Forgotten Books uses state-of-the-art technology to digitally reconstruct the work, preserving the original format whilst repairing imperfections present in the aged copy. In rare cases, an imperfection in the original, such as a blemish or missing page, may be replicated in our edition. We do, however, repair the vast majority of imperfections successfully; any imperfections that remain are intentionally left to preserve the state of such historical works.

Forgotten Books is a registered trademark of FB &c Ltd.
Copyright © 2017 FB &c Ltd.
FB &c Ltd, Dalton House, 60 Windsor Avenue, London, SW19 2RR.
Company number 08720141. Registered in England and Wales.

For support please visit www.forgottenbooks.com

1 MONTH OF FREE READING

at

www.ForgottenBooks.com

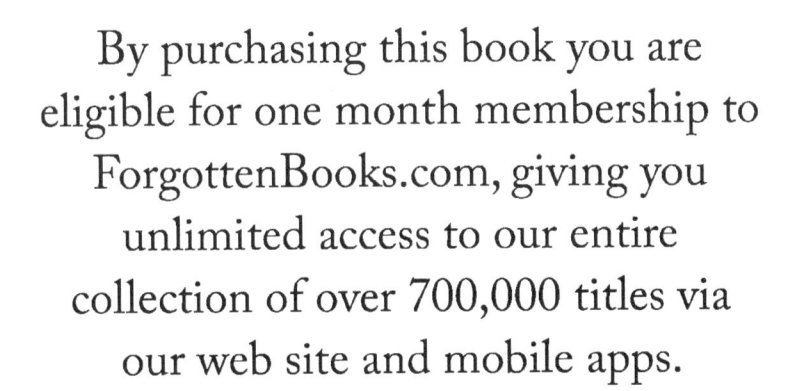

By purchasing this book you are eligible for one month membership to ForgottenBooks.com, giving you unlimited access to our entire collection of over 700,000 titles via our web site and mobile apps.

To claim your free month visit:

www.forgottenbooks.com/free13676

* Offer is valid for 45 days from date of purchase. Terms and conditions apply.

English
Français
Deutsche
Italiano
Español
Português

www.forgottenbooks.com

Mythology Photography **Fiction**
Fishing Christianity **Art** Cooking
Essays Buddhism Freemasonry
Medicine **Biology** Music **Ancient Egypt** Evolution Carpentry Physics
Dance Geology **Mathematics** Fitness
Shakespeare **Folklore** Yoga Marketing
Confidence Immortality Biographies
Poetry **Psychology** Witchcraft
Electronics Chemistry History **Law**
Accounting **Philosophy** Anthropology
Alchemy Drama Quantum Mechanics
Atheism Sexual Health **Ancient History**
Entrepreneurship Languages Sport
Paleontology Needlework Islam
Metaphysics Investment Archaeology
Parenting Statistics Criminology
Motivational

EPITOME

OF

POST-BIBLICAL HISTORY,

FOR

JEWISH-AMERICAN SABBATH-SCHOOLS.

Adapted from the German of Dr. David Leimdoerfer, and considerably Enlarged.

BY

SIGMUND HECHT,
Minister of Kahl Montgomery,
MONTGOMERY, ALA.

CINCINNATI.
BLOCH & CO., PUBLISHERS AND PRINTERS.

Entered according to Act of Congress, in the year 1882, by
BLOCH & CO.
In the office of the Librarian of Congress, at Washington.

CONTENTS.

		PAGE.
PREFACE,		3

PART I. — ANTIQUITY.

CHAPTER.
i.	Israel Under the Greeks—Alexander the Great,	5
ii.	The Ptolemies,	6
iii.	Judea a Syrian Province,	8
iv.	The Maccabees,	11
v.	Jonathan and Simon,	14
vi.	The Jews After Simon—Sanhedrin,	15
vii.	Sanhedrin at Jerusalem,	17
viii.	John Hyrcanos,	18
ix.	The End of the Hasmoneans,	20
x.	Herod,	22
xi.	Hillel and Shammai,	24
xii.	The Roman Procurators,	26
xiii.	Destruction of Jerusalem,	28
xiv.	Rabbi Jochanan ben Saccai and His Disciples,	30
xv.	The Jews After the Destruction of the Second Temple,	32
xvi.	Bar Cochba—The Fall of Bethar,	33
xvii.	The Ten Martyrs,	35
xviii.	Rabbi Akiba, His Disciples and Colleagues,	37
xix.	Rabbi Jehuda Hanassi—Amoraim,	41
xx.	Israel After Hadrian's Persecutions,	43
xxi.	The Talmud,	45

PART II. — THE MIDDLE AGES.

i.	The Jews in Persia, India and China,	49
ii.	Islamism,	50
iii.	The Caraites,	51
iv.	The Jewish Chazares,	52
v.	The Gaonim,	53
vi.	The Unhappy Fate of the Jews,	56
vii.	The Friends of the Jews,	62
viii.	Jewish Life and Work,	64

ix.	Solomon Ibn Gabirol,	67
x.	Jehuda Halevi,	68
xi.	Abraham Ibn Ezra,	69
xii.	Moses Maimonides,	70
xiii.	Ramban, Nachmanides (R. Moses b. Nachman),	74
xiv.	Don Isaac Abarbanel,	74
xv.	Rashi (Solomon ben Isaac),	76
xvi.	Isaac Alfasi (R. Isaac b. Joseph Alphes),	79
xvii.	Celebrities in Germany,	80
xviii.	Mysticism—Cabalah,	83
xix.	Benedict (Baruch) Spinoza and Gabriel (Uriel) Acosta,	85
xx.	Manasse ben Israel,	87

Part III. — MODERN TIMES.

i.	The Emancipation of the Jews in France,	89
ii.	The Jews in Holland and Belgium,	91
iii.	The Jews in Germany,	92
iv.	Moses Mendelssohn,	93
v.	The Jews in Austria,	98
vi.	The Jews in other European States,	99
vii.	The Jews in Asia,	103
viii.	The Jews in Africa,	105
ix.	The Jews in Australia,	106
x.	The Jews in America,	107
xi.	The Great Jewish Societies,	109
xii.	Religious Tendencies,	113
xiii.	Jewish Institutions for Learning,	116
xiv.	Jewish Celebrities,	121
xv.	Statistics,	123

Conclusion—Our Duty in the Present and for the Future, — 125

Chronological Table, — 129

PREFACE.

IN the following pages I desire to lay before the teachers and pupils of Jewish-American Sabbath-schools an adaptation from the German Post-Biblical History of Dr. David Leimdoerfer, Rabbi at Nordhausen. The same reasons that induced the author to publish his little book in German prompted me to attempt its reproduction in the English language.

A post-biblical history, adapted for the use of our Sabbath-schools, a history containing in the smallest possible compass the outlines of Israel's history, was a want long and keenly felt; for while many of our American teachers and scholars have labored zealously and faithfully in the field of biblical literature, and have given us many a valuable and useful text-book on biblical history, they have neglected to supply our schools with a suitable one on post-biblical history.

From year to year, however, it becomes more and more manifest that the present mode of religious instruction is inadequate, and in a great measure responsible for the religious indifference of our young. Children leave school too soon (at fourteen or fifteen). They have, at best, indifferently mastered the biblical history. That there is something behind, that the history of their people, after the close of the biblical annals, is fraught with valuable information, with sublime lessons and with examples worthy of emulation; *that* they know not, they suspect not. Thus they grow up, ignorant of that which, if known by them, would fill them with pride for Judaism and make them its warm supporters and defenders.

These reasons are of sufficient weight to plead earnestly for the general introduction in our religious schools of a course on post-biblical history, which again necessitates a suitable text-book, one that, by the brevity of its style and the completeness of its contents, would recommend itself to teachers and pupils.

In writing these pages, I have adopted and closely followed the plan of the learned Dr. Leimdoerfer, who selected his material most happily; and only where I found his accounts and statements too brief, *i. e.*, brief at the expense of clearness, I have consulted the work of Dr. Kaiserling in making my additions.

The chapter on "Jews in America," with all that belongs to American Judaism, being treated by Dr. Leimdoerfer only *en passant*, I have considerably enlarged. In writing this chapter, I used the Census Report issued by the "Board of Delegates" and the printed council proceedings of the several conventions of the U. A. H. C.

Fondly hoping that this little book may find favor in the eyes of those for whom it is intended, that it may be productive of that good to achieve which I undertook the work, and that it may satisfy a just criticism, I commend it to the teachers of Hebrew-American congregational schools, whose suggestions and corrections I solicit.

S. HECHT.

Montgomery, Ala., November, 1881.

Part I.

ANTIQUITY.

I.—ISRAEL UNDER THE RULE OF THE GREEKS.—ALEXANDER THE GREAT.

At the death of Nehemiah, Palestine was still under Persian vassalage, and remained in that state for about a century longer. But the Persian dynasty was overthrown 336 B. C., and Alexander the Great, King of Macedonia, became master of the situation. The victorious Greek soon after attacked and besieged Tyre, the capital of Phœnicia, which offered obstinate resistance for several months. While before Tyre, Alexander deputed messengers to Judea, to collect the tribute due. The High-priest Jaddua, who at the time stood at the head of affairs, and to whom the request for troops and provisions was made, refused both on the plea of loyalty to the Persian crown. Alexander was very much enraged at this, as he thought, insolent answer of the Jewish high-priest, and threatened a severe visitation of his wrath upon the inhabitants of Judea. Just then Tyre fell, after a most gallant struggle and heroic resistance, and Alexander marched upon Jerusalem. The high-priest, fearful of the possible disastrous results, now sought to propitiate the mighty conqueror, the terror of the world, and resolved upon a peaceful solution of the vexed question. Considering "discretion the better part of valor," he went out to meet the advancing conqueror. At the head of a solemn procession, composed of priests in their priestly vestments and of many prominent men, clad in white, Jaddua in his pontifical robes approached the dreaded conqueror with salutations of peace and submission. At the sight of this imposing procession, Alexander's wrath was appeased, and discovering the name of God engraven upon the plate of gold which encircled the head-gear of the high-priest, he returned the salutation and fell prostrate before the name of God. Amid the mute amazement of his generals and the loud rejoicing of the Israelites, Alexander, at the side of Jaddua, proceeded to the city. Arrived at the temple, he ordered sacrifices to be brought for him, and was very gracious to his new subjects. He granted the Jews the full and free exercise of their religion, and exempted them from taxes on every seventh year (Shemitta). Out of gratitude for such generous treatment, the Israelites throughout the realm named every boy born in that year Alexander. However, they clung faithfully to their ancestral faith, notwithstanding their good fortune, and when Alexander, after the conquest of Persia, resolved on the rebuilding of Babylon and the Belus Temple, demanded the assistance of the Jews in that work, they represented to him the injustice of his demand, as conflicting with his promises, it being contrary to their religion to assist in building a heathen temple. Alexander recognized the justice of their appeal, and, approving of their loyalty to their God, he revoked his order.

II.—THE PTOLEMIES.

In the year 323 B. C., Alexander suddenly died, at the age of thirty-two. His vast empire was divided among his generals, Syria and Judea becoming the portion of Seleucus

(Nicator.) Seleucus was friendly disposed toward the Jews, granting them equal rights with the Greeks. During his administration (311 B. C.) a new era, called after him the Seleceudian era, was introduced. Dissensions arising soon thereafter among the rulers of the small principalities, Judea fell into the power of the Egyptians, ruled by the Ptolemies, who for about one hundred years exercised their power over the Jews. During the reign of Ptolemy Soter, or Lagi, the civil and ecclesiastical affairs were in the hands of a high-priest, appointed by the King. The selection of that high functionary, however, was not always a happy one; unworthy men being often admitted to that exalted and dignified office.

Ptolemy II., Philadelphus, was a man of liberal education, and a lover of literature. It is related of him that he once found a copy of the Hebrew Bible in his library. Eager to learn its contents, he arranged for the translation into Greek of that book. In a gracious letter, accompanied by many costly presents, he requested the High-priest Eleazar to send him some able and learned men, who, under his own personal supervision, could translate that mysterious book. Eleazar, promptly complying with the request of the King, sent seventy two men (six from each tribe) to Alexandria, who discharged their duty to the full satisfaction of Philadelphus. That translation has been preserved to this day, and is known by the name Septuagint, LXX. (translation of the seventy).

Ptolemy III., Euergetes, was likewise well disposed toward the Jews. Not so, however, his son and successor, Ptolemy IV., Philopator, who persecuted them most bitterly. His hatred against the Jews was engendered by their peremptorily refusing him admittance into the Holy of Holies of their sanctuary. No one but the high-priest had access to that place, and he only on the Day of Atonement. Notwithstanding this, Philopator forced his way into the sanctuary; but ere his purpose was accomplished he suddenly fell into a swoon, and had to be carried away in a state of unconsciousness. He no sooner had recovered from this spell, when he instituted a systematic persecution of the Jews. He first removed them from all public offices, next denied them their rights, thirdly reduced them to the lowest class of citizenship, and lastly he demanded that they abandon their faith. Although a compliance with this request would have secured for the Judeans the favor of the king, yet they were resolved to bear the worst rather than become faithless to their God. Ptolemy, imbittered by their refusal, now sought to punish them in a manner unheard of before. He gave orders to bring the obstinate Jews to Alexandria and to place them in the Hippodrome. Here the Jews were to meet their fearful doom, by having set upon them a number of intoxicated elephants. The dreaded moment came. At the sight of the maddened beasts, that seemed ready to crush them under their feet, the intended victims raised a cry of terror, which strangely affected the elephants, for instead of crushing the Jews they turned against the spectators and trampled many of them under foot. Philopator, baffled at every point, began to see his injustice and to repent of it; but it was too late; the Jews had been wounded too deeply, the outrage perpetrated upon their holiest feelings was felt by them too keenly; they could never forget it, and longed for an opportunity to shake off the hated Egyptian yoke.

III.—JUDEA A SYRIAN PROVINCE.

The opportunity which the Jews sought to rid themselves of their Egyptian masters offered itself sooner than they had anticipated. Philopator had touched their most sensitive point; that they vividly remembered, even after that tyrant had died, in consequence of his intemperate habits, and

Ptolemy V., Epiphanes, had ascended the throne. This new king was a mere child when he assumed the reins of government, and this circumstance accounts not only for the renewal of the attack, which Antiochus III., the Great, had unsuccessfully made upon Ptolemy Philopator, but also for the ease with which the Syrian king now succeeded in wresting Judea from Egypt and making it tributary to Syria. The Jews would readily and cheerfully have transferred their allegiance from Egypt to anyone; but toward Antiochus, the lineal descendant of Seleucus Nicator, they felt themselves particularly attracted. Nor did they have any reason to regret the change until a later period. For Antiochus treated them liberally, accorded them religious privileges, and recommended them to the governors of his provinces as most loyal subjects. Under his benignant reign, which lasted thirty-seven years, they enjoyed the blessings of peace, prosperity and freedom. Seleucus (Philopator), the son and successor of Antiochus III., pursued the same policy toward his Jewish subjects and treated them with kindness and consideration. Seleucus (Philopator) was succeeded by his brother Antiochus IV., Epiphanes (the Illustrious), also called Epimanes (the Madman). With the accession to the throne of Syria of this tyrant, a reign of terror began for the Jews. The cruel persecutions and the heartless oppression which the unfortunate sons of Israel suffered under this king beggar description, and surpassed by far the worst treatment they ever experienced at the hands of Philopator in Egypt. The first act of his, affecting the Israelites, was the deposition of the worthy and pious High-priest Onias III., whom he supplanted by Jason for the consideration of a few talents of silver. But Jason did not long enjoy the honors of his office, being replaced by his brother, Menelaus, who offered the king a still higher price. The consequence was that this unprecedentedly high-handed dealing brought about an insurrection, which was succeeded by the most deplorable consequences. These mercenary high-priests, by the grace of Antiochus, without the least appreciation of their high dignity, turned from their people, neglected their duties and became votaries of Greek art and Greek customs, and of heathen practices. Their example was contagious, and the people, following their teachers, likewise became recreant to their duty. In the midst of this demoralization, Antiochus acted in a high-handed manner. He fell upon Jerusalem, robbed the temple, killed thousands of Israelites and commanded the abolition of the Jewish worship, to the last vestige. Every observance peculiar to the people of Israel was interdicted, the violation of the Sabbath was enforced, the reading of the law was made an offense, the scrolls were torn and burnt. Forbidden meat was given them to eat, with threats of the severest penalties if they refused obedience; in fact, every Jewish law, ceremony and custom was to be repealed, set aside or ignored under penalty of death. Upon the altars swine were sacrificed and the sanctuaries were polluted. Throughout Judea the Israelites were forced either to apostatize or die. Many indeed died rather than depart from their religion. History has preserved the names and heroic deeds of many martyrs of Antiochus' wrath, prominent among whom are those of Eleazar, an old man of ninety years, who even scorned to simulate faithlessness to his God, though he could thereby have saved his life, and of Hanna, a pious mother in Israel, who saw her seven sons die before her eyes, one after the other, amid the most horrible tortures, and who afterward exclaimed: "O my sons, tell your Father in heaven that Abraham was willing to bring his one son as an offering, but that I have offered seven;" whereupon she, too, died, glorifying the name of God with her expiring breath.

IV.—THE MACCABEES.

At Modin, near Jerusalem, there lived a priestly family, of the race of the Hasmoneans, the head of which was Matthias, the son of the High-priest Jochanan. He was the father of five sons, Jochanan, Simon, Juda (surnamed Maccabi), Eleazar and Jonathan. To this venerable and pious family Antiochus deputed one of his generals, with the order to introduce idolatry in Modin. That emissary was commanded to make the most tempting promises to Matthias, in order to win him over to his side, justly thinking that his example would be followed by the rest. But neither promises nor threats availed with the old man, and this was the definite answer he returned to Antiochus: "I and my house shall remain faithful to our God." Seeing a Jew approaching the heathen altar to worship and sacrifice upon it, Matthias, old as he was, transported with indignation, rushed upon the apostate and slew him at the foot of the altar. Herewith the signal was given for a general uprising. Matthias and his sons called upon all true sons of Israel to gather around them and to leave the city. Those men, few in number, withdrew into the neighboring mountain recesses, from whence they carried on a sort of guerilla warfare. With wonderful courage and heroism they fought for their faith, punished the faithless and chastised their pursuers. During the first year of the revolution Matthias died. Before his death he assembled all his sons around him and strictly charged them to maintain their cause fearlessly and to trust in God. He appointed Simon, as the wisest, to be their counselor, and Juda, the bravest and boldest, to be their general. (The name Maccabi has been explained in many different ways; the most probable of the various opinions is that Maccabi is derived from "maccab," hammer, and the initials of the device emblazoned upon their flag: מי כמך

באלים יהוה, "Who is like unto thee among the mighty, O God?"). The sons mourned their loss, and by their subsequent deeds proved best how they honored his memory and respected his words.

With rare heroism Juda led his small army, and with unexampled bravery he attacked the numerous hosts of the Syrians. His own example and his eloquent words tended to inspire his followers and to fill them with zeal for their cause—the cause of their religion—that no danger, however great and threatening, could destroy. The ravages of Appolonius, who brutally massacred the innocent inhabitants of Jerusalem, he stopped by killing the Syrian general and defeating his army. Seron, governor of Coelesyria, who next took command of the Syrian forces, was defeated at Beth Horon; a third army of over 47,000 men, led by Nicanor and Gorgias, were routed; while Lysias, who commanded a fourth army of 60,000 men, was defeated at Beth Zur with heavy losses. After these brilliant feats, Juda turned his attention to Jerusalem, which was still garrisoned by Syrian troops. Here also he succeeded, he recaptured the citadel, drove out the enemy, and took possession of the Temple. To cleanse it and to rededicate it to the service of the One God was his main care. Amid popular rejoicing he erected a new altar in place of the one that had been desecrated by the impure sacrifices, cast out the statue of Jupiter that had defiled the sanctuary, and pure offerings of thanksgiving once more burned upon the altar. During the succeeding eight days, these festivities were observed, in commemoration of which joyous event the Israelites have instituted the feast of Chanuka (dedication of the temple) during the eight days succeeding the 25th of Kislev, with the lighting of special tapers and appropriate prayers.

But the battle was not over yet. It was but a short respite before a new and more terrible outbreak. Antiochus, however, did not live to see the defeat of the Israelites. In the year 164, while attempting to plunder a temple at Elymais, he was repulsed, a humiliation which deeply wounded him. About the same time he received intelligence of the success of Juda and the defeat of his armies, which aggravated a disorder he had contracted, and while breathing vengeance against the Judeans he was seized with a fit of madness and died on the way to Palestine, suffering fearful agonies. Juda now applied to Rome for assistance, but from that moment fortune seemed to have forsaken his arms, and he suffered defeat until he died. Antiochus Eupator, the son of Epiphanes, was but nine years old when he ascended the throne, with Lysias as regent. An immense army was equipped to crush the successful Jewish insurgents. In this engagement Eleazar, the brother of Juda, lost his life, being crushed to death by an elephant. Demetrius Soter, the son of Seleucus Philopator, dethroned and put to death young Eupator and usurped the throne. This new king continued the war of extermination against the Jews and was powerfully supported by the treacherous High-priest Alkymus. The decisive battle was at hand. Bera, a small place, was the battle-field. Juda Maccabi had but 800 men to oppose the tens of thousands of Syrians. Yet he dared oppose them. He fought like a lion. It was a long, desperate and heroic struggle, but he was finally overpowered. He died the death of a hero (160 B. C.) His bravery and heroism have become proverbial. He was tenderly lifted from the blood-stained battle ground, and, amid the lamentations and wailings of all Israelites, his brothers buried him in Modin; Juda Maccabi was a man whose equal is rarely if ever found, and the fears of the bereaved brethren and people, of what might be the results of his death were well founded.

V.—JONATHAN AND SIMON.

Two of the brothers of Juda, Eleazar and Jochanan, had already preceded into the mysterious hereafter that heroic Maccabi who was the pride and the glory of his people. Jonathan and Simon alone were left to continue and to complete the great work for which their aged father, even at the brink of the grave, had taken up arms, and for which their three brothers had bled and died. Jonathan succeeded Juda and displayed great bravery and tact in the protracted war for liberty. The grandson of Antiochus Epiphanes, Antiochus Theos, now ruled Syria, and during his reign Jonathan attained high honors. But it was only a passing ray of sunshine, closely followed by a dark and disastrous cloud. Tryphon, the regent of the young King Theos, who had secretly planned the overthrow of his monarch, with the object in view of supplanting him on the throne, sought to tempt the unsuspecting Jonathan, and by flatteries and promises induced him to open the gates of Ptolemais (Acco). Justly fearing this favorite of the king as a mighty obstacle in the execution of his vile scheme, he treacherously caused his death. For fourteen years, from 160 to 146 B. C., Jonathan had skillfully and wisely defended the cause of his people, when, with him, another prop of the Jewish nation fell.

Simon, now the only remaining son of Matthias, succeeded his youngest brother, and for him it was reserved to regain the full autonomy and independence of Judea, which had been lost since the destruction of the Solomonian temple under Nebuchadnezzar. He dispersed the Syrian garrisons in the fortresses of Judea, he fortified Mt. Zion and forced the Syrians to recognize the *independence of the Jewish State*. Twenty-five years of anguish, of bloodshed and of sorrow had passed since the day on which the handful of zealous men, led by Matthias, had retreated to the mountain fastnesses for the purpose of defending thence their sacred rights, until Simon was recognized prince and ruler of Judea. A new era now began, the Simonian, replacing the Seleucedian, which ceased after a period of about 166 years — from 311 to 146 B. C. His titles of prince and high-priest were ratified and made hereditary by popular voice; in commemoration of which event coins were struck, some of which have been preserved to this day.

Now that the swords rested in their sheaths and peace smiled around, Simon devoted his energy and wisdom to the introduction of useful institutions. He called into existence the Sanhedrin, a judiciary which proved a strong protective wall for the cause of the frequently-endangered religion. But, as if preordained that none of that noble Hasmonean family should die a natural death, this wise and noble man, too, met not only with an unnatural, but a most revolting end. In the eighth year of his peaceful and prosperous reign, while traveling through Palestine, with the object in view of personally investigating the condition of the country, and of improving where improvement was required, he came to Dok, a city near Jericho, where at the house and by the instigation of his own son-in-law he was treacherously murdered.

(Jochanan had died long before, having been killed in a contest with the Arabs.)

VI.—THE JEWS AFTER SIMON.—SANHEDRIN.

Under Grecian rule, the Jews gradually adopted the language and the knowledge of their masters. Jewish doctrine, connected and united with Greek philosophy and the contemplation of the world, called forth the so-called Apocrypha, *i.e.*, excluded writings—writings which have not been admitted into the collection of the twenty-four holy books (Canon). To these apocryphal writings belong the Books of the Maccabees, Book of Wisdom, Book of Sirach, Judith, Tobias, Baruch, and others. But with the language and knowledge of the Greeks they (the Jews) also acquired their bad habits and immoral practices. To the great misfortune of the people, the high-priestly office was degraded by godless men — men who, like Jason, loved heathen pleasures better than their faith, and whose pernicious example had a like effect upon the masses, who, following their guides, soon caused the decadence of religion. Fortunately for the Israelites, they never lacked men who stood up for the maintenance of the divine laws, who called into existence institutions for the dissemination of light, and who aimed at the fear of God and the practice of faith. Such an institution they had in the great Sanhedrin, which, it is said, originated under Ezra, but had remained inactive and unobserved until then. The men of the great Synod collected and completed the Canon; they introduced the "Sch'ma Israel," and they are the authors of the first and last three benedictions of the "Sh'mone Esre," and of the prayer after meals. Many of those pious and God-fearing men have uttered beautiful and instructive sentiments and morals, of which many are preserved to this day, and collected in the Ethics of the Fathers, a part of the Mishna. Thus, for instance, Simon the Just said: "The world rests upon three things, viz., law, instruction and charity." Antigonus of Socho said: "Be not like servants who serve their masters for the sake of reward."

The same body advocated also the erection or establishment of houses of prayer and instruction. Such places of assembly for the purpose of devotion and instruction were called synagogues, in which three times daily prayers were offered—Shacharith, morning; Mincha, vesper, and Marib, evening prayers. On the Sabbath and festivals, and also on the second and fifth days of the week, corresponding with our Mondays and Thursdays, portions of the Pentateuch were read aloud before the assembled congregations. At the time of the Syrian oppression under Antiochus, when the scrolls of law were either burnt or defiled, they read some portions of the Prophets in place of the "Tora." This substitute is known even to this day under the name of "Haftora," or closing reading. The people, affected by Greek culture, having become strangers to their own language, the Tora, and later also the Prophets, had often to be suitably translated and commented upon. Thus the Targumin, *i. e.*, translations and sermons, came into practice. The scribes and savants were highly esteemed by the people and replaced the prophets of old.

VII.—SANHEDRIN AT JERUSALEM.

The men of learning, whose main object was the perpetuation of the Jewish faith, did not merely seek to cultivate the study of the law, or to develop and thus to hand it down from father to son (tradition), but they likewise understood jurisprudence, and established a court of law, with the power and duty to enact religious ordinances and to decide in legal cases. This tribunal, consisting of seventy-one men, was known by the name of Sanhedrin, and had its seat at Jerusalem. In this body was vested the highest power, to which even the high-priests and princes were subject. They decided and determined upon war or peace, and had jurisdiction over life and death. The chief of that court was called Nassi, prince or patriarch; second to him stood the Ab-Beth-Din, or chief justice. Members of that august body were specially sanctified by a ceremony called "Semicha." This ceremony was performed by the Nassi, and consisted in laying his hands upon the head of the new member. The sessions of that body were held in the great hall before the Temple, and were open to the public. Besides decisions in questions of faith and law, the Sanhedrin also determined the beginning of the moon (moled), new moon, by which the festivals were appointed and celebrated. Men especially charged watched for the first appearance of the moon, which was thereupon quickly communicated from place to place, either by couriers or by a fire lit upon some hill-tops. Under the direction of the Nassi there was also the high-school at Jerusalem, in which lectures and debates upon religious subjects were had, and from that high-school graduated judges and teachers. Besides the great Synhedrin at Jerusalem, there existed minor Synhedria, consisting of twenty-three members, in every large country congregation; while at small places the judiciary consisted of three persons, composing a Beth-Din, or minor court.

VIII.—JOHN HYRCANOS.

After the death of Simon, his son, John Hyrcanos, so called from having defeated Kendebaios the Hyrcanian, became prince and high-priest. During his reign Judea prospered and increased, both in territory and in magnificence. Intestine strifes in Syria diverted the enemy's attention from Judea, and the Judeans improved this time and opportunity in regaining all the cities that they had previously lost. The Samaritans and Idumeans were subjugated by John Hyrcanos, who forced them to embrace Judaism, an act of intolerance which bore bitter fruits. The Samaritans, originally heathen colonists whom Salmanassar, after the overthrow of Israel, had colonized in that territory, and especially in Samaria, although familiar with the biblical writings of the Jews, nevertheless, praticed idolatry, and could not, therefore, be recognized as Jews. Moreover, they had calumniated and antagonized the Jews since the days of Ezra and Nehemiah. On being forbidden to take part in the erection of the second temple, they had built one on Mt. Gerizim, where it is said they worshiped a dove. The breach already existing between the Jews and Samaritans thus became widened until every trace of a common faith vanished. That temple was destroyed by John Hyrcanos, who conquered Samaria and forcibly converted her inhabitants. In like manner he chastised the Idumeans, who had been hostile to the Jews. By his victories, Hyrcanos extended his dominions, which soon rivaled in extent the territory of Solomon.

Toward the end of his reign, however, he excited the popular will against him. On one occasion, namely, while celebrating one of his victories, he requested his invited guests te tell him if he ever had been recreant in the discharge of his duties. Thereupon one of the assembled men arose and said: "No, but you ought to resign the crown of priesthood and be satisfied with your worldly power, because you are the son of a bondwoman, and as such not lawfully entitled to be high-priest." Hyrcanos, deeply wounded because of this insult offered to the memory of his mother, ordered a strict investigation of the matter, and when it was found that the accusation was unfounded, and that his mother never had been a slave, he punished the traducer, cut loose from the Pharisees and became a Sadducee. In the thirty-first year of his reign he died, leaving five sons: Aristobulus, Antigonus, Alexander, Absalom, and one whose name has been lost. Aristobulus, the eldest, was to be high-priest, while to his wife he bequeathed the crown. Aristobulus, however, was a very ambitious man, and not content with the crown of priesthood, aimed also at the princely diadem. To accomplish his end he resorted to the most brutal and cruel means. His brothers, with the exception of Antigonus, were thrown into prison, and his mother he caused to perish of hunger. His wife, Salomé, supported him in all his vile schemes, and finally persuaded him to order the execution of his brother Antigonus. Tortured by remorse and lashed by his own outraged conscience, Aristobulus died after the short reign of but one year.

IX.—THE END OF THE HASMONEANS.

Salomé, the widowed queen of Aristobulus, soon after her husband's death opened the prison doors, behind which her brothers-in-law had been confined, and bestowed her hand in marriage upon one of them, Alexander Janai, in whose hands she placed the reins of government. Alexander's whole reign was characterized by warfare, which was attended by changing fortunes. His love for war, however, caused him to shed rivers of innocent blood. Nor was he in great favor with the people, he being a Sadducee, as his immediate predecessors had been, while the masses clung to the teachings of the Pharisees.

Simon ben Shetach, a brother of Queen Salomé, who was a Pharisee and had founded a Pharisaic Synhedrin and several academies, was compelled to flee to escape the ill-will of his royal brother-in-law. Nor were his fears unfounded, for Alexander caused 800 Pharisees to be put to death, while he wreaked his vengeance most signally upon 5,000 rebels. But the end of this cruel king had come. While beleaguering Ragaba, he died, after a reign of twenty-seven years, leaving behind him two sons, Hyrcanos II. and Aristobulus II. Salomé, who, as the wife of Alexander, was called Alexandra, now sided with the Pharisees, the more so since it was the wish of her dying husband that she should seek to propitiate that party at whatever sacrifice. Simon ben Shetach was now recalled, and he, with Judah ben Tabbai as Synhedrial chief, promulgated religious laws for the fortification of the faith. Alexandra gave her regal sanction to those laws. She ruled nine years after her husband's death, appointing Hyrcanos II. her successor and high-priest. But Hyrcanos did not enjoy his title in peace nor for a long time. For Aristobulus

II., his brother, jealous of the preferment, rebelled against and defeated him. Hyrcanos, a weak-minded man, took the defeat good-naturedly and withdrew from public life, while the more ambitious and fiery Aristobulus assumed the throne and pontificate. For three years following all was peaceable and quiet, and might have remained so but for the intervention of Antipater, an Idumean, full of ambition and craftiness. He allied himself to the defeated Hyrcanos, who had lived contentedly in his retirement, and succeeded in arousing within him the desire of regaining the lost throne.

Aristobulus applied for help to Pompey, the Roman general, who was invading Syria at that time, but Hyrcanos likewise sought the same influence in behalf of his cause. Pompey seemed to incline toward the elder brother, and Aristobulus, of course unwilling to abide by that decision, assumed a warlike attitude toward the Roman. Pompey, finding Aristobulus on the war-path, marched against Jerusalem, held by Hyrcanos' brother, and took the city on a Sabbath, 12,000 people losing their lives. In the heat of the battle, and while the sword destroyed and cut off many a valuable and innocent life, Pompey visited the temple, where the priests, unaffected by the ravages without, continued their several functions. This true devotion touched the general, and he gave orders not to interfere with the priests nor with their offices. Aristobulus was taken prisoner and carried to Rome to grace the conqueror's triumphal entry into the city.

Judea lost in part her independence, and became a Roman tributary, with Hyrcanos as Ethnarch. Hyrcanos, old and feeble, soon thereafter transferred his political power to that wily and ambitious Idumean, Antipater, who succeeded in winning the favor of Rome and of Julius Cæsar. Thus the Hasmoneans lost the throne forever, and their loss was caused by the feud of two brothers.

X.—HEROD.

The crafty Antipater had succeeded in gaining unlimited influence with the Ethnarch; in fact, he was the power behind the throne. Under such circumstances it was easy for him to provide bountifully for his four sons. One of them, Herod, he appointed Governor of Galilee, and the son, profiting by the example of his father, knew how to increase his power and to rise step by step, until finally he became master and ruler of all Judea. While yet the governor of a small province, he showed the bent of his character. He defied the authority of the Sanhedrin, which no one ever had the presumption to do before. Nor did his greater power tend to make him weaker. Soon after his coronation he displayed a bitter hatred against the members and partisans of the Hasmonean family, although he had married Mariamne, the beautiful grand-daughter of Hyrcanos II., and by this alliance had become related to the Hasmoneans. Feeling himself insecure as long as any of that family lived, he caused the death of the aged Hyrcanos, while he disposed of his young brother-in-law, the sixteen-year-old brother of Mariamne, in a most brutal manner. This youth he induced to go bathing with some of his mercenaries, who were instructed to drown him. The unsuspecting victim of Herod's perfidy went into the water, where, under the cover of approaching darkness, his head was held under the water till he expired.

For this act of inhumanity, which became known in spite of all the precaution which Herod had taken, he was summoned to Rome to defend himself before a tribunal. Bribing his judges, he secured his acquittal. During his absence, Salomé, the worthy sister of Herod, heartlessly removed all the surviving members of the Hasmonean family, except one, a young child, that was miraculously saved, and Mariamne, the beautiful and truly beloved wife of Herod, who was, however, soon among the victims. On leaving for Rome he left orders that in case of his conviction Mariamne should be killed, because he would not allow her to become the wife of another. The man who was charged with this odd mission, though bound to secrecy, acquainted Mariamne with his master's orders, in consequence of which revelation the returning husband was coldly received by his wife. This behavior did not escape the notice of the sister of Herod, who was not slow in pouring into her brother's ears the poison of jealousy, completing the evil designs formed in her brother's absence.

Herod, lashed into fury, accused his innocent wife of faithlessness, and the Synhedrin, misled by the evidence of perjured witnesses, found her guilty and pronounced the solemn verdict with the sentence of death.

But no sooner was the sentence executed than Herod regretted his rash act and was well-nigh distracted. His deeds of violence not only caused him the keenest pangs of a remorse-stricken conscience, but engendered the hatred of the people, and this hatred grew with his deliberate violation of the most sacred precepts of religion. But, once steeped in blood, he could not return, but pursued steadily his bloodthirsty career. Finding the Sanhedrin opposed to him, he had all of them killed except two (Shemaya and Abtalyon.)

He appointed and removed high-priests according to his pleasure, and in order to further win and secure the favor of the Romans, he aimed at Romanizing all Palestine, by bringing about an amalgamation of Jews and heathens. In honor of the Roman Emperor he built the city of Cæsarea, theaters for gladiatorial combats, while at the portico of the temple he placed the Roman eagle, which was considered a violation of the Jewish religion. He died in the seventieth year of his age, amid the most agonizing pains of a long and torturing malady. The people throughout the country regarded this as a punishment from God. Immediately before he expired he ordered one of his sons to be killed, and requested his sister that as soon as he should have expired, she should assemble all the nobility of the land at Jericho, and have them killed. In that barbarous manner he wished to secure a popular mourning at his funeral. This order, however, was not carried out, and the day of his death became one of joy, as also each anniversary thereof for many years thereafter. (About the last year of Herod's reign, Jesus, the founder of the Christian religion, was born at Nazareth of Jewish parents.)

Herod left a will, according to which Judea was to be divided between his three sons, Archelaus, Antipater and Philip. These divisions remained separate until Agrippa I., grandson of Herod, reunited them, having secured the country and the title of king from the Emperors Caligula and Claudius in 41 A. C. In the year 44 the country became a Roman province, and was governed by Roman officers.

XI.—HILLEL AND SHAMMAI.

The Jewish state was terribly convulsed, and the birth of the daughter religion, Christianity, did in nowise contribute to the re-establishment of the disturbed equilibrium. This unsatisfactory condition induced the learned men and scholars of the people to provide against the infringement upon the Mosaic Law. In order to carry out that plan they impressed upon the popular mind the traditional laws that had been promulgated since the Babylonian exile. These laws formed a fence (Geder) around the laws of Moses. Those men, rarely gifted with intellect, became rabbis, *i. e.*, teachers and guides in Israel, and established schools in which religion and science were cultivated. Among those who acquired particular celebrity were Hillel and Shammai, two teachers, who, in those troublous and dark days, contributed vastly to the maintenance of Judaism, if, indeed, they were not chiefly instrumental in its preservation.

Hillel was prominent, not only because of his great learning and depth of thought, but also on account of his gentle, kind and humane character. He was a lineal descendant of David, but so poor when he came to Jerusalem from Babylon that he was forced to earn a scanty livelihood by cutting wood. Driven by a thirst for knowledge, he desired to attend the lectures of the academy, where Shemaya and Abtalyon lectured, but unless he could fee the porter he could not gain admission. Consequently he was compelled to devote the greater part of his income to purchasing the right of a student at the academy. And when once, on a cold winter day, unable to satisfy the doorkeeper, he was refused admission, Hillel climbed up to the flat roof of the school-house, where he could hear the lectures of the rabbis. There he became so absorbed in thought, and so rapt was his attention, that he took no notice of the snow, which fell thick and fast, and soon covered him entirely. He was found on the following morning, numb and almost helpless, when he was brought into a warm room. By proper treatment he soon regained perfect health and strength, and when the details of his adventure became known, he was enrolled among the regular attendants and received gratuitous instruction. By his diligent application he soon gained the rank and the name of a rabbi, and in course of time was advanced to the office of Nassi. His wisdom and learning were wedded to rare patience, modesty and love of mankind. Of the many instances that could be mentioned in proof of these exalted virtues, one may find a place here. A heathen, whom Shammai had rudely turned away, came to Hillel, expressing the desire of becoming a Jew, provided he could be taught the doctrines of Judaism while standing upon one leg. Hillel, instead of spurning him, patiently submitted even to this seemingly insolent request, and said: "'Love thy neighbor as thyself;' that is the essence of our religion; all the rest is amplification, which thou wilt learn later."

Shammai, although of quite a different disposition—he being of an irascible, impetuous and at times violent temper—was a man likewise distinguished by penetration and profound learning. Both Hillel and Shammai were at the head of large schools, which often expressed opinions widely different from each another. As a rule, however, the views of Hillel and his school (Beth Hillel) prevailed. His dignified post as Nassi of the Sanhedrin, Hillel maintained for a great number of years, even after he had completed the unusual four-score years of his life. The Nassiship became hereditary in his family for ten generations. Of those sons and descendants of Hillel may be mentioned prominently his son, Gamaliel I., who established the great and celebrated academy at Jabne (Jamnia), and introduced many useful ordinances and regulations, and his grand-son, Simon ben Gamaliel, who was the author of the saying: "The study of the Law is not the principal thing, but the practice thereof."

XII.—THE ROMAN PROCURATORS.

After the death of Herod, there was such widespread dissatisfaction in Palestine, both among those that wished to govern and those that were to be governed, that Rome assumed direction of affairs in Palestine, by appointing procurators.

The will of Herod making a division in Judea did not tend to pacify the troubled elements.

These officials, almost without exception, oppressed and maltreated the Jews to such an extent that every change of procurator was from bad to worse.

Pontius Pilate, about 37 C. E., was one of those demons

in human form who mercilessly trampled upon the most sacred feelings of the people, whose life, property and honor were to him alike of no consideration. And yet, cruel, heartless and unfeeling as he was, he found his superior, in all those qualities which make man detestable, in the last of the procurators, Florus. This tyrant fairly drove the Jews to despair, but then they made front against him, and bravely fought for their rights. Gallus, the Syrian governor, who came to the assistance of Florus, was repulsed by Simon ben Gioras. This momentary success aroused new hope in the hearts of the Jews, and they boldly determined to shake off the Roman yoke; the more so since they expected to find a powerful ally in Artaban, the Parthian king. The warlike party, the Zealots, were in the majority, and outvoted the peace party, which was impotent, while those hotheaded patriots fanned into flame the embers of rebellion against the Romans. Nero, who was then Emperor of Rome, on hearing of this insurrectionary movement, sent his general, Vespasian, against the Jews. But their bravery never forsook them; as not only Vespasian, but even Titus and Trajan, could attest. The decisive battle was fought at Jotapata, a fortress in Galilee. This fortification was held by Josephus Flavius, the celebrated historian. Vespasian devised many ingenious plans and resorted to all kinds of bold stratagems, and threw up ramparts, but the Jews threw them down and killed the men employed in their construction. For forty-seven days that small fortress withstood the attacks of 60,000 Romans, but at last it fell, and then only by the treachery of a deserter; 40,000 Jews lost their lives, and 12,000 were taken prisoners. Josephus fled to a cave, where he found forty other men. He asked them to surrender to the Romans, but finding them resolved rather to die, he pretended to share their bravery. It was decided by lot who were to be the victims, and who the executioner.

He managed that he and another were spared to the last. The two then went forth, threw themselves at Vespasian's feet, were pardoned, and received rich presents. Vespasian returned to Rome to receive the crown of the Cæsars (69 C. E.), and sent his son Titus to continue the war in Palestine.

XIII.—DESTRUCTION OF JERUSALEM AND THE TEMPLE.

In the spring of the year 70 C. E., Titus marched upon Jerusalem with a great army. The bitter feuds that had raged in the city between the Zealots and the peace party, and which had tended to considerably weaken their forces, now ceased, and both parties united for a bold and desperate attack against the Romans. The siege was protracted, the most daring attacks were executed and the most ingenious plans carried out by the Romans; with rare boldness and bravery the Jews withstood them. This resistance exasperated the Romans, who now applied every possible means to capture the fortified suburb, Bethesda, which they succeeded in doing by the employment of warlike engines. After Bethesda was taken, the Jews were asked to surrender, but they refused, preferring the most unequal contest to a debasing capitulation. The Romans proceeded to storm the city with their engines, successfully repeated their attacks, and after two months they took Acra, the fortress near the temple mount, which, being surrounded by a high, double wall, resisted for some time the implements of destruction brought into play by the Romans. In the meantime, the famine in Jerusalem had assumed great proportions; indeed, the worst was at hand; there were no provisions of any kind to be found in the city, and the poor, unfortunate inhabitants of Jerusalem died by the hundreds of hunger. The streets became filled with the unburied dead; this produced pestilence, which claimed untold victims. At this pass Rabbi Jochanan ben Saccai, a disciple of Hillel, raised his voice in favor of a surrender of the city, but in vain; his words were disregarded; the Zealots were stubbornly determined not to yield, but to fight as long as there was breath in them. The fatal moment drew nearer and nearer. The Romans, driven to madness by the futility of their efforts, at last set fire to a tower filled with wood. This tower, being near the wall, communicated the fire to it, and now all was lost. Life and property were set at naught; one thing alone, the sanctuary, they wished to save, but in vain; the Roman hirelings forced their way into the city, where a fearful carnage ensued. Like furies, the Romans only desired to destroy and to kill; one of them hurled a burning torch into the sanctuary; it caught fire, and Mt. Zion, with its beautiful temple, became a smoking ruin, Jerusalem a heap of ashes. This sad calamity occurred on the anniversary of the destruction of the first temple (by Nebuchadnezzar, about 600 years previously), on the ninth day of the fifth month, Ab, which day up to now is the most important historical day of mourning and fasting for the Israelites. The Jewish State had ceased to be. Fully 1,000,000 human lives were lost in this battle and 100,000 Israelites were sold into slavery. Crowned with victory, Titus returned to Rome to celebrate his triumphs. The holy vessels of the temple were exhibited as trophies, triumphal arches were erected, and the most eminent Israelites, among whom was Simon ben Gioras, were tortured and executed. In addition to all this, coins were struck to perpetuate this brilliant feat of the Roman arms. The coin bearing the inscription, *Judea Capta*, represented the conquered Judea by a widow lamenting beneath a palm-tree, and scorned and derided by a Roman. We can not, of course, assign the cause of this great calamity with any degree of precision, though it may safely be assumed that the godlessness and still more the intestine conflicts and feuds of the Jews of those days were in a great measure responsible for that terrible misfortune.

XIV.—RABBI JOCHANAN BEN SACCAI AND HIS DISCIPLES.

Judea was lost, the Jewish State had ceased to exist; Judaism, however, lived; the Jewish religion was saved, and will ever be protected by the Eternal, lest it perish. Close upon the heels of the political catastrophe, men arose who were the saviors of their faith. Such a man was Rabbi Jochanan ben Saccai, of whom mention has been made already, and who, a faithful disciple of Hillel, had acquired vast knowledge, extensive learning and noble virtues. While yet the siege of the Romans lasted, he counseled peaceful submission, but finding his words disregarded, he determined upon helping his brethren in a different way. He caused the report to spread that he was sick; he then feigned death, was put into a coffin, as he had previously arranged with his friends and disciples, and thus succeeded in being carried without the gates of the city. He sought the Roman general, Vespasian, to request of him some favors. The plan, so oddly yet ingeniously conceived, was successfully carried into effect. The Roman's confidence was won, and that all-powerful general granted the peaceful rabbi the privilege of establishing an academy at Jabue (Jamnia).

This seat of learning soon flourished, and out of its walls came forth the wisest men and teachers. Indeed, it may safely be assumed that the school at Jabne, and other similar institutions erected about the same time, were the safeguards, supporters and upholders of Judaism. Rabbi Jochanan ben Saccai also re-established the Sanhedrin, and conferred the dignity of Nassi upon Gamaliel II., the son of the former Nassi. This dignitary was very strict in the discharge of the functions of his office; he brought about union and harmony in Israel, whereby he materially strengthened its condition, and watched carefully over the divine service. Rabbi Jochanan ben Saccai enjoyed the respect and the veneration of the whole people until his death, which occurred at a very advanced age, when he was sincerely mourned, and distinguished by the name, "Light of Israel." Of his disciples, he preferred five in a special manner. Of those five, two deserve particular mention, viz., Rabbi Eleazar ben Hyrcanos and Rabbi Joshua. Up to the age of twenty-eight, Eleazar could neither read nor write. His father had destined him for a farmer's life, but Eleazar's tastes inclining him toward learning, he left his home and sought Saccai, that he might become his disciple. In a short time Eleazar had made progress with giant strides, and soon became a celebrated man. His father, who at first did not know where his son was, went in search of him, and came to the seat of the academy. He heard of his son's presence there, and resolved to disinherit him. But finding how high a rank he occupied among the rabbis, the father relented and offered to make him sole heir of all his property; but Eleazar declined this proposal and declared: "I am not in search of material possessions; I strive for perennial goods."

Rabbi Joshua, on the other hand, was a witty and highly-cultivated man, so much so that he was a welcome visitor at the royal board, though he was but a blacksmith by trade and of very homely exterior. The princess often engaged him in lively conversation, and made him the object of her playful raillery. Thus she once asked him banteringly: "Tell me, Rabbi, how comes it that so great a mind dwells in so ugly a form?" In place of a direct answer, he asked her: "In what kind of vessels do you keep your wine?" "In earthen vessels, of course," she replied. "That is wrong," said Rabbi Joshua; "you ought to keep it in golden vessels, by all means." She did so, and before long the wine was spoiled. In this manner he proved to her that external beauty is not always a sure index of internal excellence. Rabbi Joshua was very highly esteemed by the people, and, despite his low station in life, he ranked with, and perhaps above, the patriarch, Gamaliel II., with whom he once for a short time lived in discord because of some disagreement.

Rabbi Jochanan ben Saccai was undoubtedly the founder of the regular school in Palestine; and, following his excellent example, others after him erected and established schools in Tiberias, Sepporis and other places, thus creating a permanent home for religion and science and securing their stability.

XV.—THE JEWS AFTER THE DESTRUCTION OF THE SECOND TEMPLE.

The national existence of Israel having been terminated by the Roman conquests in Palestine, the Jews emigrated to other countries, as, for instance, to Egypt, where they found their brethren who had previously settled there under the Emperor Caligula. The Jewish community of Alexandria produced a man of superior attainments and warm impulses, who, both by writing and speaking, worked faithfully in the interest of his people. It was the well-known historian and philosopher, Philo, who on one occasion repaired to Rome to defend the Jews against the unjust accusations of their bitter foe, Apion. Jewish congregations and settlements also sprang up in Persia and Babylonia. From Asia and Africa they spread to Europe, and wherever they lived they were united by one strong tie, that of their faith, to which they rigidly adhered; and by harmonious and united efforts they progressed and prospered. In every congregation there was a place for communal devotions and a school for the instruction of the young. As citizens of the respective countries which they had selected for their habitation, they sought to avoid anything that could militate against them, they conscientiously performed their duties as citizens, and, following the recommendations of the Prophet Jeremiah, they prayed for the welfare and prosperity of their adopted country and its rulers. The Jews living in the Occident placed in authority over them a spiritual head, with the title of Nassi; those in the Orient selected a spiritual head, to whom they applied the title of Resh-Gelutha, *i. e.*, Exilarch. Both the Nassi in European countries and the Resh-Gelutha in the Asiatic provinces lived in princely style and enjoyed high respect and veneration. They superintended all religious institutions, and their opinions had great weight with the civic authorities and with the government in general. The office and dignity of Exilarch remained intact up to the twelfth century.

XVI.—BAR COCHBA (130 C. E.).

The life of the Jews under the Romans was a very bitter one. The emperors succeeding Titus with few exceptions continually oppressed their hapless victims. So great were the hardships they had to bear that even after that disastrous defeat in the year 70 they attempted twice to defend themselves. These emperors who, by their immeasurable cruelty, challenged resistance, were Trajan and Hadrian. While Trajan was engaged in war with the Parthians, the Jews in Cyrene and Cyprus rose up in resistance to the hostile Greeks; but Hadrian, then general-in-chief of the Roman armies, defeated them. Trajan's successor on the throne was Hadrian, who, on assuming the imperatorial dignity, seemed well-disposed toward the Jews, or at least more friendly toward them than his predecessor had been. This favor, however, was, as a stray sunbeam on a cloudy day, of but very short duration. Soon he changed his manner and became a tyrant in the " worst and fiercest construction " of that word. He inhibited the exercise of the Mosaic law under penalty of death. At the same time (about 130 C. E.) a man of rare bravery and eloquence appeared and soon became prominent. His name was Simon, and considering himself the God-chosen Messiah, pretended to be able to liberate his brethren and to break the yoke of Rome. With reference to the phrase, "there steppeth forth a star out of Jacob" (Numbers xxiv. 17), he assumed the name "Bar Cochba," "Son of the Star." The people, sorely oppressed, and wishing, hoping and praying for the advent of the Messiah—the Redeemer promised and foretold by the Prophets—were easily led to the acceptance of and belief in this pretender, who, by the way, might have been quite serious and sincere in the belief in his own Messiahship; the more so as his entire bearing and deportment were calculated to inspire every one. Thus he soon gained many supporters. Nearly a half-million of soldiers enlisted, in the firm hope of speedy deliverance; nor was the opportunity or occasion for action long in coming. It happened in this wise. A couple who had just been married was, according to the custom then prevailing, preceded by some persons carrying chickens. The Romans despoiled the bearers of their fowls, whereupon the Jews fell upon them to defend their rights. Hadrian, hearing of this, sent his general, Rufus, with a great army against them; but Bar Cochba repelled the attack, advanced, reconquered Jerusalem, several fortresses and about 900 smaller places. The Jews were rejoiced at this brilliant victory, and in commemoration thereof they struck some coins, bearing the device: "For Israel's liberty." But this joy was short-lived. Rufus was defeated, but not the Romans, who were only the more iufuriated and bent upon the severe punishment of those fierce and irrepressible Jews. Severus took charge of the Roman hosts as commander-in-chief, and Hadrian placed at his command a very numerous army. The manner of procedure adopted by Severus was unlike that of his predecessors. He did not engage in open battle, but by means of cutting off supplies and by light skirmishes he reduced the insurgents, and, with the exception of the fortress Bethar, held by Bar Cochba, the Romans regained all they had lost under Rufus. For one entire year Bethar withstood the hostile attacks of the beleaguerers, but finally (135 C. E.) even this fortress and stronghold became weak and was forced to surrender, because of the prevailing scarcity of food. Among the 100,000 victims whom this last war had claimed was also Bar Cochba, who latterly was sarcastically called Bar Cozba, son of falsehood. The fall of Bethar, more than any previous occurrence, blighted and removed every hope of shaking off the supremacy of the Romans.

XVII.—THE TEN MARTYRS.

Hadrian's tyrannical character became daily more manifest. His inhuman proceedings against the Jews grew into ferocious persecution, which had for its object not only the extermination of the hapless Jews, but was also directed against their religion. Another Antiochus, he issued an edict prohibiting the reading or preaching of the Tora, making such occupations criminal offenses, punishable by the death of the transgressor. But what is human law compared with the divine! and never yet could nor did a tyrant successfully domineer over the powers of conscience and conviction. Israel never was so forsaken as to lack true heroes in the hour of greatest danger. And there were such men in Israel at that unfortunate time—men of character and consideration, who had nothing so much at heart as the study of the divine law. Ten of those men, recognizing the greatest danger for Judaism—nay, the total destruction of their faith —in a compliance with and obedience to the emperor's unjust behests, bade him defiance, and thus chose death for their portion, when life could only be gained by the surrender of life's holiest aim. Those ten men are known in history by the name of the ten martyrs. Their names are: Simon ben Gamaliel, the patriarch; Ismael, the priest; Rabbi Akiba, Rabbi Chuzpith, Rabbi Juda ben Baba, Rabbi Chanina ben Teradyon, Rabbi Eleazar ben Shemuah, Rabbi Jesebeb, Rabbi Chanina ben Hachinas, and Rabbi Juda ben Damas. The agonies and tortures to which these men were exposed are indescribable, and their painful death is almost without a parallel in history. When one of them, Rabbi Akiba, was yet in prison for the violation of the imperial decree, he was visited by one Papus, who asked for the reason of this stubborn resistance. Rabbi Akiba said: "Listen while I tell you an anecdote. A fox once walked upon the bank of a river abounding with innumerable fish. The fishermen were busily angling for them, and the inhabitants of the water were consequently in great commotion. 'What is the cause of all this confusion?' asked the fox; he received the answer that they were hurrying from the fishermen's nets and hooks. 'Come out of the water, then,' said the sly fox, 'and they will do you no harm.' But they answered him: 'Art thou really the wise fox? Thy advice belies thy shrewdness. For if here, in our element, we are in danger of our lives, how much more would this be the case upon dry land, to which we are not accustomed?' Thus I say to thee, Papus: If in the study of the Law, which is our element, we are endangered, what would be the danger if we abandoned it? Surely thou art not the wise man I thought thee to be." On being led to his death, he recited portions from the Tora. The flesh was torn from his body with iron combs, and in the midst of his sympathizing disciples, he alone retained his firmness. When, moved to tears by the cruelty inflicted upon their beloved and respected master, they exclaimed, "Alas! is this the reward of thy piety?" he answered, "Certainly; all my life I have been wishing for an opportunity to prove my love for God, not only with my heart and might, but also with my soul, with my life; and now that I have that opportunity, should I cowardly seek to evade and not rather persist in my sanctification for God?" With the words "Adonay Echod," "God is one," he expired. Rabbi Chanina ben Teradyon died a death as terrible as that of Rabbi Akiba. While teaching publicly in defiance of Hadrian's order, those fiends, the minions of the Roman tyrant, wrapped him in a scroll of the Law, which they set on fire, and to prevent the rapid burning and to increase his tortures, they put wet wool upon his breast from time to time. Amid excruciating pains, yet with prayers upon his lips, he died. In former years, while the anniversary of the destruction of Jerusalem (ninth day of Ab) was yet universally observed, those ten martyrs were always mentioned in a song of lamentation. (Congregations that still observe the ninth day of Ab recite that chapter during the morning service of that day.)

XVIII.—RABBI AKIBA, HIS DISCIPLES AND COLLEAGUES.

Rabbi Akiba, one of the ten martyrs mentioned in the preceding chapter, was a star of particular brightness on the horizon of learning. Tradition accords him a life of 120 years. He was about fifty-five years old when Titus destroyed Jerusalem, and lived until about 135 C. E. Up to his fortieth year he had lived in utter ignorance, in the capacity of a shepherd to a wealthy man of Jerusalem, named Calba Sabua. Between him and his employer's daughter there sprang up a mutual love, and his ignorance was the only obstacle that stood between him and the possession of the woman he loved. She had promised to become his wife if he should succeed in gaining some fame for his learning. The forty-year-old Akiba was almost driven to despair; believing his time for learning to have passed forever. But he once accidentally noticed a stone before a spring which had become somewhat hollowed by the water which constantly dropped down upon it. The sight of this stone set him to thinking, and he said: If a stone can be impressed thus by water, why should not my heart be impressed thus by the divine word? Quickly resolved, he sought the academy of Rabbi Joshua, learned with great alacrity, and soon became not only a thorough and apt pupil, but a revered master and one of the greatest teachers. His disciples are said to have numbered some 24,000. Thus distinguished and revered, he returned to Jerusalem and married the daughter of Calba Sabua. Rabbi Akiba possessed the rare gift of lucidly and ingeniously explaining the most insignificant passages of Scripture, and to his wisdom was wedded the fear of God. He adopted as his motto, "Whatever God does is well done;" and he often had occasion to convince himself of its truth.

His many sayings, maxims and aphorisms, as well as a great number of narratives and anecdotes by and of him, are preserved in Hebrew literature. His disciples, probably owing to their vast numbers, could not at first agree. It so happened that once, after the Passover festival, while the Omer days were counted, a pestilence broke out among them, which, however, ceased on the thirty-third day after the second night of the Pesach.

In commemoration of this strange and unfortunate event, the days of the Omer, with the exception of Lag B'omer (thirty-third day of Omer), were characterized as days of mourning, during which no kind of enjoyment was permissible. Marriages were not contracted during that time, nor was any pleasure indulged in. This custom was preserved for a long time, and even to-day there are many who still adhere to it. After the tragic death of Akiba, briefly mentioned in the former chapter, his disciples and colleagues undertook the maintenance of his schools and the erection of others. Such schools or Academies flourished in Sepporis, Tiberias, Usha, etc. Among his contemporaries there were:

1. Nahum, the Gamsu man, so called because he was used to accept any untoward circumstance in perfect resignation, always saying " *Gam su l'toba*," " this also is for good." This man, a teacher of Akiba, was born in Gimsu, a place not far from Lydda, and it is supposed that his watchword, Gamsu, was adopted from a slight change of the name of his native place. In his old age he was visited by many mishaps. He first lost his eyesight and then his limbs became paralyzed. He used to tell those that came to visit him that his sufferings were a just punishment for his evil deeds, for that once when on his way with rich presents for his father-in-law he had been asked for alms; he had let the poor man wait until he had unloaded his asses, and in the meanwhile the poor man had died.

2. Rabbi Meir, a prominent scholar, who possessed the happy faculty of teaching in a manner which never tired. He embellished all his lectures with beautiful legends and witty sayings. His memory was prodigious. It is related of him that being at a place in Asia Minor, the congregation of which had no Meguillah (Esther), he wrote it for them from memory, without omitting a single letter. His disciples, with whom he stood in high regard, eagerly listened to all his utterances, and his colleagues said of him: " When Rabbi Meir instructs, it is as though he uprooted mountains and ground them against each other;" or, " Whoever touches Rabbi Meir's words must improve in wisdom." He disliked any blind following of the words of even the most eminent persons. He favored and strongly recommended individual research and examination, and gave utterance to that sentiment by saying: "Look not at the vessel, but ex-

amine its contents; there may be new pitchers full of old wine, and old pitchers that contain not even new wine." Rabbi Meir deprecated any hurried recitation of prayers and insisted upon their being devoutly and reverentially offered. He said: "Better little prayer with devotion than much without it." In matters of religion he was very exact, and considered it wrong in anybody to marry one without religious knowledge. Yet he was very liberal, and always preferred a heathen who studied the divine law to an Israelite, or even to a priest, who neglected that study. His teacher was Rabbi Elizar ben Abuya (known in history by the name of Acher, the other, because he became a skeptic with regard to the dogma of the unity of God, and people did not wish to mention his name). Rabbi Meir never withheld his regard or veneration from that teacher, despite of his infidel doctrine.

3. Rabbi Simon ben Jochai, who for thirteen years lived in a cave in order to escape the persecutions of the government. During those years he was engaged in literary pursuits, and the book "Sifri" (commenting upon the fourth and fifth books of Moses) is ascribed to him. Some even consider him the author of the "Sohar," a cabalistic work. At an advanced age he journeyed to Rome to prevent a renewal of the proscriptive laws and edicts of Hadrian, and was favorably received by the Roman authorities. Besides these there are to be mentioned:

4. Rabbi Ismael, author of the "Mechiltha" (commentary on Exodus).

5. Rabbi Eleazar Chisma, who studied mathematics and astronomy.

6. Rabbi Jose ben Chalaphta, who, though a tanner by trade, was a profound student of the Law.

7. The cooper, Rabbi Judah ben Ilai Hachassid, who lived

so plainly that he wore no other garments except those made from the stuff spun by his wife; and,

8. Rabbi Juda, son of Rabbi Simon ben Gamaliel, called the Holy, who was by a peculiar circumstance permitted to grow up with a son of Hadrian, Marcus Antoninus, who in later years, when emperor, preserved and proved his friendship for the companion of his youth.

XIX.—RABBI JEHUDA HANASSI—THE AMORÄIM.

After the persecutions of the Jews by Hadrian, the Sanhedrin, presided over by Simon ben Gamaliel II., attained high authority. Babylonish congregations, although governed by the Exilarch and under his control, recognized, nevertheless, the resolutions and decrees of that Sanhedrin. Simon ben Gamaliel II. was succeeded by his son, Rabbi Jehuda Hanassi, the one mentioned in the preceding chapter. He was also called "the Holy One," or "Rabbi." The birthday of this illustrious scion of the house of Hillel was the day on which Rabbi Akiba was executed by Hadrian's edict. A great part of his considerable fortune he devoted to the support of poor students, to enable them to continue their studies. But notwithstanding that he was celebrated for his learning and highly respected by all, he was modest. His greatest work, for which his memory is cherished to this day, was the collection and compilation of the "Oral Law," or tradition, known as the Mishna. He died at the age of sixty, universally lamented and mourned, especially by the great number of disciples whom he had fitted for their career. Those disciples of Rabbi Jehuda Hanassi who devoted themselves to the explanation of the Mishna were called Amoraim, *i. e.*, speakers, commentators, in contradistinction to the rabbis preceding them, who were known by the name of Tannaim, or Mishna teachers.

The most prominent of the Amoraim were:

1. Rabbi Jochanan, the founder of an academy at Tiberias, over which he presided until his death. He was a man of prepossessing exterior, but had the misfortune to lose his ten sons in the prime of their life. When his last son had died he carried one of the bones of his body constantly with him, in order the more effectively to console anyone similarly bereaved. The Jerusalem Talmud, which appeared at 370 C. E., was his work.

2. Rabbi Simon ben Lakish, a disciple of the former, and remarkable for his mental acumen. He was of gigantic power and build and strictly just and upright in all his dealings.

3. Aba Areka, an intimate friend of Artaban, the last king of Parthia. He founded a school at Sura, in which he gathered around him some 1,200 disciples. For nearly 800 years Sura remained a prominent seat of learning. Aba's disciples venerated him so much that they called him only Rab, by which name he is known in the Talmud.

4. Samuel, the friend of Aba, became the religious chief of Babylonia in the year 237, after the death of the latter. Samuel was not only a great Talmudist, thoroughly conversant with Halacha (jurisprudence), but possessed a considerable knowledge of medicine, while as an astronomer he was so eminent that he could boast of himself: "I am as well acquainted with the streets and walks in heaven as with those in Nahardea."

5. Rabbi Abahu, a man of great wealth, an extensive slave-owner and manufacturer of veils. He understood Greek thoroughly, and gave his daughter instruction in that language. Some of his contemporaries thought very ill of him on that account. His clear and logical reasoning, his accomplishments and dignified bearing, made him a favorite with the emperor and the most prominent men of Rome.

6. Rabbi Huna, for forty years teacher at the school of

Sura. Next to the study of the laws of God, he was an eminent agriculturist, who did not disdain to work his fields alone. In later years he acquired considerable wealth, which he very judiciously applied to the support of indigent students.

7 and 8. Two keen commentators.

9 and 10. Rabina and Rab Asha, publishers and compilers of the Babylonian Talmud (375–427 C. E.).

Besides these there may also be mentioned Rabbi bar Nachmeni, Joseph ben Chiya and Rabbi Papa.

Of the successors of Rabbi Juda Hanassi, his grand-son, Juda, the prince, Nassi, deserves particular mention. He was surrounded by princely pomp and addressed with the title of Highness, even by the Roman government. Concerning the practice of the oral law, he promulgated several measures and orders to facilitate its exercise.

XX.—ISRAEL AFTER HADRIAN'S PERSECUTIONS.

The two centuries succeeding the reign of Hadrian were strongly marked and clearly distinguished from the times before and following those two hundred years. The Jews had bravely yet unsuccessfully struggled against the Romans, and the successors of Hadrian permitted them to live in undisturbed quietude and peace. Marcus Antoninus, Marcus Aurelius and Severus granted them many privileges and liberties. Even Valerius and Diocletian, two Romans who did not treat with any consideration the daughter religion of Judaism—who rather dealt harshly with and bitterly oppressed Christianity—even they did not oppress the Jews. But times changed, too soon for the welfare of the Jewish race. It was at the time when the Roman rulers became Christians that they interpreted their new faith to consist in cruelty and opposition to the Jews. The founder of the Christian doctrine, a Jew himself, strictly obeyed the

Mosaic law, and adopted as the basis of his new law and religion the commandment: "Love thy neighber as thyself," as found in III. B. M. 17, 18. This new departure proved of great advantage at first, inasmuch as many heathens were thereby converted to the belief in one God. But many of the priests and church-fathers that stood at the head of this new movement soon effected a complete rupture between this and the Jewish law. Nor did they stop there, for they tried to make the Jews suspected and persecuted them. The first Roman emperor who was converted to and embraced Christianity, showed his appreciation and admiration for his religion by suppressing the Jews and burdening them with heavy taxation. Julian was not so unreasonable. In opposition to the unwarranted persecution of the Jews by the clergy, he commanded the rebuilding of the temple and of Jerusalem. Toward the Nassi, Hillel II., he was very gracious, and in a letter directed to him he addressed that high functionary as brother. In that letter the Emperor Julian requested that the Jews should pray for him, that God might grant him victory over the Persians, after which (he said) he would unite with them in proclaiming the glory of one God.

The rebuilding of the temple was begun, but suddenly there came a fire from out of the rubbish, which most probably was the work of some malevolent incendiary; yet superstition became very strong, and no one dared to continue the work. Julian was succeeded in turn by Honorius and Theodosius II., who, unlike their liberal predecessor, were cruel and full of hatred against the Jews. Theodosius caused the massacre of 1,000 of them in Alexandria, which resulted in the impoverishment of that city.

XXI.—THE TALMUD.

Rabbi Jehuda Hanassi had collected the Mishna, and by committing it to writing saved the great treasure from being lost. But it was short and often epigrammatic in its passages, and an urgent necessity made itself felt to enlarge and comment upon it. To meet this want, the religious schools and academies undertook the task of adding the Guemara to the Mishna. Guemara is called the explanation and elucidation of the Mishna. Both Mishna and Guemara are known by the name of Talmud. Of this great work there are two distinct editions—the Jerusalemic (Hierosolomyton) Talmud, edited in 370 by Rabbi Jochanan, a disciple of Rabbi Jehuda Hanassi; and the Babylonian Talmud, edited by Rabina and Rab Asha, the head of the school at Sura (375–427 C. E.). The latter contains, in sixty books, the traditional laws governing the religious life (Halacha), and the sayings, maxims, ethics and anecdotes of the individual rabbis, which they used for popular edification (Haggada). Halacha was regarded as binding and applicable to all. Haggada could be variously received and explained. Of the manner in which this gigantic work was compiled, and which it is said occupied sixty years, we are told that of the sixty books comprising the Mishna, Rab Asha took two every year, which were divided and distributed among his disciples. Every year there were two meetings, at which he delivered discourses on one of the books of the Mishna, with his explanations. They were then dismissed for five months, during which time they were to collect all they knew or had learned in the meantime; at the next meeting their works were arranged and made into a whole. The work was completed in this manner within thirty years, and thirty years longer were required to revise, correct and bring it into permanent shape. In this arduous labor Rab Asha was ably supported by Rabina.

The Talmud is divided into six great parts or orders (Seder); every order into treatises (Massecheth); and every treatise into chapters (Perek). The Halacha soon assumed the authority of the Mosaic Law; it became an object of profound study and research, which occupied the rabbis by day and by night; it quickened their thoughts, and challenged sharp reasoning; it was regarded as the fountain-head of faith and science. The Haggada again offered an inexhaustible source of popular instruction. All eagerly listened, with joyous and rapt attention, to the sound maxims which furthered virtue and the moral love of God and man.

The following selections from the Talmud may bear testimony to the beauty and depth of Talmudic ethics:

a) *From the Ethics of the Fathers (Pirke Aboth):*

Hillel:—" Love peace and pursue it; love mankind and bring them to the study of the Law." i. 12.

Shammai: — " Let the study of the Law (religion) be a fixed business of thine; say little and do much, and receive all men with an open, friendly countenance " i. 15.

Simon ben Gamaliel:—" The duration of the world depends on truth, justice and peace." i. 18.

Shemayah: —" Love labor and hate dominion." i. 10.

Levitas:—" Be exceedingly humble of spirit, for the end of man is to be food for worms." iv. 4.

Rabbi Jochanan ben Saccai:—" If thou hast learned much of the Law, pride not thyself thereat; because for this purpose alone wast thou created." ii. 9.

Zoma:—" Who is wise? He who is willing to receive instructions from every one. Who is a hero? He who subdueth his evil inclination. Who is rich? He who is content with his lot." iv. 1.

Rabbi Jehuda Hanassi:—" Reflect well on three things, and

thou wilt not lapse into the power of sin: know what is above thee, an all-seeing eye, a hearing ear, and that all thy actions are written in a book." ii. 1.

Rabbi Joshua:—" Envy, passion and hatred of mankind remove man from the world." ii. 16.

Eleazar ben Shamnah:—" Let the honor of thy scholar be as dear to thee as thy own; the honor of thy associate as the fear of thy teacher, and the fear of thy teacher as the fear of God." iv. 15.

Rabbi Simon:—" There are three crowns—the crown of the Law, the crown of the priesthood and the crown of the kingdom; but the crown of a good name is superior to them all." iv. 17.

Samuel the Younger:—" Rejoice not when thy enemy falleth, and let not thy heart be glad when he stumbleth." iv. 24. Etc.

b) *From the Talmud:*

" The ultimate end of all laws is to purify and to unite in love all mankind.— Correct thy own failings before thou admonishest thy neighbor.—Passion is at first like a cobweb or a fragile thread; by degrees it becomes a heavy rope.—Do wrong neither to thy brother in the faith nor to him who differs with thee in matters of faith.— The uncharitable is to be compared to an idolater.—The just and virtuous have a portion in the future reward, irrespective of their creed or nationality.—Why was but one man created? In order that one generation should not say to another, My father was greater than thine.—An infidel once said to Gabiha: 'Ye fools who believe in the resurrection of the dead, behold, the living die; how, then, can the dead live again?' 'Fools ye are yourselves,' answered Gabiha; 'if that which was not comes to existence, why should it be impossible for that which was to be again?'—He who possesses wisdom without the fear of God is like one who has the inner keys of the house, but not the outer ones. How can he enter it?—Unhappy is the man who, in despair, deems himself lost; unhappy he who deems himself perfect.—Prayer is the worship of the heart.—Rather than publicly expose to shame any one, suffer thyself to be cast into a caldron of fire.—Love him more who calls thy attention to thy faults than him who constantly praises thee.—The imperishable monuments of the truly pious are their good deeds.—Throw no stone into the well from which thou hast once drank.—Rather perform the meanest labor than beg.—It is a sin to give alms and boast of it before man.—The proud man is an idolater who worships himself.—Wisdom secluded within itself is like a myrtle in the desert, that rejoices no one.—As the wine goes in, the secret goes out.—It is not the place that honors the man, it is the man who reflects honor upon the place.—Modesty is a beautiful ornament of man.—When two quarrel, you may be sure that he who first stops is of the better descent.—The heart and the eye are the two agents of sin.—The myrtle remains a myrtle, even though it be among thorns and brambles.—The punishment of the liar is that his word is discredited, even though it be the truth.—Selfish love quickly vanishes; unselfish love lasts eternally."

Part II.

THE MIDDLE AGES.

I.—THE JEWS IN PERSIA, INDIA AND CHINA.

As early as the time of the completion of the Talmud, there existed many large Jewish congregations in Persia, where, notwithstanding their loyalty, they were exposed to the tyranny of the Persian rulers. Kobad, King of Persia (520 C. E.), desired to force all his subjects to embrace his religion, and, when the Jews refused, he ordered Mar Sutra, the Exilarch, to be executed on the bridge of his own city, Machusa. The Jews against the Christians, and these against the Jews, brought about a very deplorable state of affairs, which terminated in the loss of many thousands of lives.

Previous to this there had been an emigration of some seventy-two Jewish families, who settled in India, and, prospering and increasing, they remained there until 1510, in the enjoyment of peace and tranquillity. But when they were driven from their possessions in India by the Portuguese, they found refuge in Cochin, where the young men married black slaves, after they had become Jewesses. These unions produced the black Jews.

Of the Jews in China we have but very few data. So much is known, however, that there are several Jewish congregations in the Celestial Empire, that the Jews enjoy equal rights, are admitted to all offices, have synagogues surrounded by trees and Chinese tents, and speak a Hebrew mixed with Persian. Their holy writings contain thirteen books; twelve in honor of the tribes, and one as a token of reverence for Moses. They have not all the books we possess, but those books which they have are precisely like ours. In reading the Pentateuch in their synagogue, the reader stands, in a blue hat and cotton Thalith, before a desk called the "Moses' desk." The rabbi wears a sash of red silk around his shoulder. They still observe some ceremonies, but no longer understand Hebrew. They number in all about 600 souls.

II.—ISLAMISM.

The Jews, maltreated and oppressed in Palestine, settled, as we have seen, in Persia, India and China as early as the third century. Yet Arabia, adjoining Palestine, was the most welcome asylum of the fugitives. The Queen Zenobia, who, it is alleged, was of Jewish extraction, is said to have secured for them a comfortable position in Palmyra (Tadmor) her residence. In the year 274 her dynasty was overthrown, and the Jews went to Palestine. In 622, Mohammed, founder of a new religion, the Islam, conquered all Arabia. He at first treated the Jews found in Arabia with consideration, but, finding that the new doctrine which he offered them was not promptly accepted—nay, that it was positively refused—hatred sprung up in his heart, which gradually grew and became intense. Though the Torah became the source from which his book, the Koran, emanated, though he recognized next to Ismael also Abraham, Isaac and Jacob as patriarchs, and Moses as the divine prophet, and though whatever knowledge he possessed he owed to the learned

Jew, Ibn Naufel, he was, nevertheless, most intolerant against the Jews. Before his death he expressed the wish that no unbeliever or dissenter should be tolerated in the land of the Moslems. This wish or order, however, was not carried out, for his successors, the caliphs, not only tolerated the Jews, but, being recognized as the bearers of knowledge, they enjoyed their high esteem. Islamism soon spread over the whole Orient in Northern Africa. In European Turkey, Spain and everywhere the Jews lived peacefully and happily under its influence. Their schools and academies flourished and worked successfully upon every branch of science. Omar, one of the caliphs succeeding Mohammed, bestowed the dignity of Exilarch upon one Bostenai; while Ali, Omar's successor, was no less liberal and generous, granting the title of Gaon (Highness) to the director of the high-school at Sura, a title which Babylonian chiefs of schools retained until the eleventh century.

III.—THE CARAITES.

In the year 762 a new sect of Jews sprang into existence, this time in the Mohammedan State. This sect was called Caraites. Anan ben David, a man living under the caliphate of Al Mansur, aspired to the office of Resh Gelutha (Exilarch). Being unsuccessful, he formed that new sect, which, not unlike the Sadducees of former times, aimed at the strict observance of the written law of the Torah, and nothing else. In this establishment of a new sect, Anan merely imitated the example of the Moslems, in whose midst the Shi'ites were once a party rejecting the Mohammedan tradition (Sunna). The name Caraites is derived from Cara, *i. e.*, to read, and only what they read in the Bible was considered binding; they rejected, however, the traditions and the spiritual conceptions of Scripture. From the words (Ex. xxxv. 3), "You shall kindle no fire on the Sabbath day," they deduced the strict prohibition against the lighting of a candle on the Sabbath. The Shabuoth (feast of weeks) they always celebrated on a Sunday; the Shofar (cornet sound) and the Tifillin (phylacteries) they took figuratively. Up to the time of the Crusades they lived in Palestine, where they had quite a number of followers; later on they emigrated, and settled mostly in Russian provinces. About 400 of them may be found even to this day on the Crimean peninsula, at Odessa and other places. These remnants of the once numerous sect of Caraites are distinguished by strict honesty and purity of morals. Though they clung to the letter of the Law, they were spiritually active, nevertheless, and ably defended their doctrines, to which fact their comprehensive literature abundantly testifies. A Caraitic prayer-book was written by Akron ben Joseph in the thirteenth century. In 1570 a well-known Caraite was Moses Boshrazi, who is the author of a book called Matté Elohim, which contains the doctrines of faith adopted by their sect.

IV.—THE JEWISH CHAZARES.

A new Jewish kingdom, that of the Chazares, arose simultaneously with the empire in Russia. This new Jewish realm rose on the northern shore of the Caspian Sea and maintained itself during a few centuries. The Chazares were the successors of the warlike Fins, who had settled there after the downfall of the Huns, their tribal relatives. Persecuted by the inhabitants of the Byzantia and new Persian States, the Jews sought and found protection with these Chazares. The princes of that territory, also called Chazanes, respected the Jews on account of their knowledge, and they were made the interpreters in any treaty that was concluded with the neighboring rulers. In the eighth century, one of those Princes, Chagan Bulan, with his family and his highest dignitaries, embraced Judaism. The doctrines of this religion struck deep roots and were finally made a law; thenceforth all kings were to be of Mosaic faith. They were tolerant toward Christians, Mohammedans and heathens, and permitted them to remain faithful to their respective convictions or beliefs. Of the further history of this kingdom there is but meager information extant. Not until the eleventh century was the existence of such a State discovered, nor of the eleven Jewish kings who had ruled it. In 1016, the Russian Grand Prince Mietislow defeated David, the last of the Chazaric princes, whose throne was overthrown for all time.

V.—THE GAONIM.

The completion of the Talmud brought in its wake some changes, which, however, affected Judaism only externally. The dignity of school and Nassi was lowered, because oral instruction had ceased to be a necessity. Gamaliel, who was deposed from his office in 429 for reasons unknown, was the last of the Nassis or patriarchs. But neither the abolition of that office nor the completion of the Talmud interfered with the continued activity of the Jewish mind, which was rather enhanced by the efforts of the rabbins to strengthen the authority of the Talmudical code. As formerly among Persians, Greeks and Romans, so now among Arabians did the Jews acquire their language and lore. The Sabureans, that is, arbitrators, wrote many treatises on the Talmud, and besides their works there were produced many philosophical writings in the Arabic language, thus bringing about an amalgamation of profane and theological knowledge. The Sabureans maintained themselves for only about one century and their time may justly be designated as the poorest in Jewish history. After the Sabureans came the Gaonim (exalted), who under that title began to superintend and direct the Jewish academies in the domain of the Islam. They were very active in the field of literature, and many excellent works of the Gaonim period, which extended to the eleventh century, have descended to us. Although the Exilarch had become a mere figure-head, and his dignity a mere sound, while the Gaonim were vested with the powers of the former Sanhedrin, yet there were many difficulties and quarrels between the Exilarchs, who were appointed as a matter of form, and the Gaonim; and the former, in order to maintain their dignity, made free use of the Cherem (anathema), which they hurled against their antagonists.

The most prominent among the Gaonim were:

1. Rabbi Simon, of Kahira, author of a book containing ritual laws.

2. Rabbi Achai, of Shabcha, author of a collection of casuistic researches in Deuteronomy.

3. Rabbi Amram, celebrated for the order of prayers which he established.

4. Rabbi Zemach I., author of a Talmudical lexicon.

5. Rabbi Nachshon, an eminent astronomer, who issued a table for a new almanac.

6. Rabbi Saadya Gaon, undoubtedly the greatest of them all, was born in 892 at Fayum, in Egypt. This celebrated man early attracted the attention of all for the vast knowledge he possessed. He was elected academical chief at Sura at a time when Judaism was in a most critical condition, on account of the attacks made upon it by the Caraites on one side and by Christianity and Islamism on the other. These attacks were severe enough, and would have endangered, if not indeed shattered, the Jewish religion, had not this man, apparently appointed by Providence, undertaken to fight for his faith. Armed with the invincible weapons of science, he triumphantly established the excellencies of Jewish doctrines as based upon sound reason. At the instigation of his antagonists, who considered him a dangerous innovator, the

caliph deposed him from his Gaonate. But he was soon recalled, and thenceforth to his death, in 942, he worked incessantly and patiently for the welfare of his people. The mourning for this, one of the greatest men, was as sincere as it was universal. A few points of his life may find a place here. He was a man of firm character, striving after truth; his sense of justice, his candor and his true piety were genuine pearls that glitter in the diadem of his memory. At the age of thirty-six, Saadya, though an Egyptian, was chosen Gaon, a dignity which no foreigner before him had received, and at once he devoted himself to his task. Soon he had an opportunity to prove his firmness of character, and, regardless of consequences, to maintain the truth against his superior. Two years after he had assumed his dignity there was a case which required his signature as Gaon. He refused it. The Exilarch pronounced an anathema against him, and appointed another man Gaon in Saadya's place. Saadya hurled back the anathema upon David, the Exilarch, and appointed Josiah Hassan to that office. A rupture ensued, which lasted three years, when Hassan died. David fully reinstated, Saadya was compelled to flee. For seven years he lived in perfect seclusion from the world, during which time he wrote his numerous and valuable works, the first of their kind that had ever been committed to paper. Among the numerous works published by this great man, the one entitled "Emmunoth V'deoth" (faith and science) was the most important.

7. Rabbi Sherira (930–1000 C. E.), author of a history of Jewish teachers in letters, and of many theological decisions. He, too, was persecuted, and, by order of Caliph Achmed, imprisoned.

8. Rabbi Hai (997–1040 C. E.), celebrated for his opinions on religious questions and for his kindness and humanity. In him the Gaonate lost its last support, for when Rabbi

Chiskia, who succeeded Rabbi Hai, had been in office two years, Caliph Kadir had him executed without just cause, and the period of Gaonim had run its course.

From the time of the Gaonim date the first collections of the Midrash (*i. e.*, interpretation of the Bible) and many of our prayers, among them the V'hu Rachum, formerly recited on Mondays and Thursdays. While the Babylonian schools thus declined, the academies in Spain rose to eminence and became celebrated.

VI.—THE UNHAPPY FATE OF THE JEWS.

From the eleventh to the sixteenth century the Jews passed through a most lamentable and sad period. In the land of the Moslems alone they were comparatively free. In Christian lands, however, their fate was a melancholy one, indeed. The history of that period strongly resembles some copious extracts made from a high-sheriff's day-book. Hated, despised, spurned, and most unmercifully butchered. The voice of humanity was silenced, the supreme law of love proclaimed by Jesus became inoperative. Wealth, virtue, knowledge and talent, which the Jews possessed, availed them nothing. With all the purity, morality, loyalty and submission to the temporal powers, it was a crime in their eyes to be a Jew. Venturing on the street, he became an object of scorn, and was exposed to the vilification and insult of an ignorant, unbridled, merciless people. On Sundays or other Christian festivals, it was not safe for a Jew to leave his humble dwelling. The exercise of religion, their devotion, could not be held openly, but in subterranean places— in caves, or locked cellars, under the cover of night. Popes, bishops, monks, and especially kings, were hostile toward them. Whatever the Jews possessed, especially in Germany, was the property of the ruler, who could and did appropriate to himself their property at pleasure. Charles

IV., in 1349, pawned them once for 15,200 pounds of pennies, with the stipulation that should the pledges die before the amount was repayed, their property would be transferred to the creditors. Most arbitrarily did these German sovereigns deal with the Jews, whom they considered as mere chattels. Thus, for instance, Emperor Louis granted to Prince William I., in 1330, the privilege of admitting twenty-four more Jews into his estates. Such rights and privileges were at last granted to all princes who held imperial estates.

Notwithstanding all the hatred which the Jews experienced, they became indispensable to their enemies because of their wealth. Trade was their only means of gaining a livelihood, and because they were thus unjustly dealt with, and required to pay the heaviest taxes, they were by force of circumstances led to become usurers. Still, proscriptive laws were passed against the Jews; they were prohibited from taking high rates of interest, and yet even princes and prelates were at times compelled to raise money by giving the Jews as pledges their estates or holy books, robes, etc. They were rigidly excluded from every public office of trust, and yet the landed proprietors not seldom appointed a Jew to the office of supervisor. They were strictly prohibited from having Christian servants or Christian nurses; and yet this law was often violated, because the Jews paid higher wages. There was a law prohibiting the Jews from giving a party for more than twelve persons; their clothing had to be of coarse cloth; they were allowed to wear no fur except the skin of calves. Any wrong done a Jew could be made good by a trifling sum of money. Plundering, robbing them of their wealth, was a daily occurrence in every country. In Magdeburg, Germany, in 1261, on the Feast of Tabernacles, the archbishop had all the wealthy Jews arrested, and a ransom of 100,000 marks was put upon them. In France, in 1182, they took their money and drove them out of the country. Under Louis IX., in 1230, they were sold from hand to hand, like any article of barter. In England they were likewise a football of fate, now banished, now recalled, now protected and now oppressed. Cromwell favored them, and during his protectorate they were recalled and tolerated. The treatment they experienced was nothing in comparison with the chase after Jewish souls. But while the Jews were often forced to submit to baptism, they sometimes offered obstinate resistance. Thus they followed the new converts in Frankfort up to the entrance of the church, to oppose their baptism, and out of 204 only twenty-four were baptized; the other 180 were killed. The greatest oppression and most fearful persecution came in the wake of the Crusades, which began in the eleventh century. The worst kind of fanaticism characterized the age, and murder was an every-day occurrence.

Falkmar Gottshalk and Count Emigo enrolled crowds of followers in Saxony and Thuringia, and started out to murder the Jews. In Cologne the houses and places of worship of the Jews were pulled down. In Worms they were compelled to become converts, but many preferred becoming suicides. In many countries on the Rhine mothers killed their own children to save them from the bloodthirsty mob. In Trier most of the Jews were killed. Many became public converts, while in secret they observed with devotion the Jewish faith. In Spire and Mayence the blood of the Jews deluged the cities and cried for vengeance. The Crusaders, however, who were little better than highway robbers, were defeated by the Bulgarians, the agents of retributive justice.

In the Second Crusade the Jews in several French cities suffered the agonies of their brethren in Germany, the victims of the First Crusade. Incited by the monk Rudolph, the mob plundered, abused and massacred them. The unheard of charge of infanticide was preferred against the

French Jews. They had killed—thus the unreasonable and violent soldiers of the cross averred — a Christian child, to use its blood for their Passover celebration, as if the use of blood had not been strictly forbidden by their law. Yet it was maintained, and many of the wrongly accused were burned alive. Similar charges were raised in Germany, where Conrad III. and several bishops sought to protect them. In Wurzburg, Munich, Nuremberg and many other cities, there flowed rivers of Jewish blood. But they did not stop here. When the charge of infanticide had lost its power, they advanced another accusation, and positively asserted that the Jews had desecrated and defiled the *host*, and again they were accused of poisoning wells, and by such means the fury and excitement against the Jews were kept up. In Switzerland, in Austria and in Bohemia, systematic persecutions of the Jews were witnessed. In Nordhausen, a city in Germany, they show to this day the so-called Jew towers, with tombstones from the thirteenth century, where the whole congregation, 600 families, with their rabbi, suffered death by fire to escape compulsory baptism.

In the Third Crusade, the Jews of England in general, and particularly those of London and York, suffered many hardships. They offered ransom, but this only postponed the butchery until the money was paid. King John caused the teeth of a Jew to be extracted by force, and the poor victim was not released until he had paid 10,000 marks in silver; and the yellow badge, which Pope Innocent III. had ordered the Jews to wear on their clothes as a sign of their race, was likewise adopted for the British Jews. The Dominican monks tore Jewish children away from their parents and brought them up in the Christian faith. In the year 1290, all the Jews were banished from England, but even this emigration was attended by severe trouble. When the vessel carrying the banished Jews across the Thames, came to a sandbank, the captain caused them all to disembark, and left them there, saying, with scorn in his words and looks: "Moses, who brought you through the Red Sea, may bring you upon dry land."

The sufferings of the Jews in Spain baffle any attempts at description. In Seville, Valencia, Toledo, Barcelona and Cordova, there were but two alternatives, either cruel death or baptism. The Inquisition, a clerical court composed of the most fanatical judges, instituted by Ferdinand and Isabella for the extermination of heresy in the Catholic Church, largely and fiercely affected the Jews. And when Ferdinand V. and Pius II. heard of the secret religious meetings of these Jews who had outwardly submitted to baptism, that bloody court caused the execution of 2,000 of them, while many were thrown into dungeons. Thomas Torquemada, the great Inquisitor, succeeded in securing the passage of a decree of banishment, promulgated by Ferdinand V. and Isabella, by which all Jews were excluded from Spain. Only four months' time was given the unfortunate Jews, during which they could dispose of their estates and property; after that time, however, they were forbidden, under penalty of death, to remain or be seen in Spain. Don Isaac Abarbanel, a celebrated Hebrew scholar, prostrated himself before the Queen, imploring her to revoke the cruel edict of banishment, and to permit his brethren to remain in a country which they loved, and to which they were so warmly attached. When words and entreaties were exhausted, he offered the covetous king 30,000 ducats toward defraying the expenses of the Moorish wars. During this audience, and while these negotiations went on, Torquemada, crucifix in hand, entered the room in which Abarbanel pleaded before the royal pair, threw the crucifix upon the table, and, exclaiming angrily, "Judas Iscariot sold his master for thirty pieces of silver; your majesties are about to do it for 30,000 ducats; here he is, take him and barter him away," left the room. This decided the fate of the Jews. The decree was enforced. About 300,000 of them were obliged to leave their beloved homes (1495 C. E.). They emigrated to Africa, Italy, Turkey and Portugal. Misery and want, sickness and famine, claimed the lives of many thousands of them.

Nor were they better treated in Portugal, from whence, in 1506, they were banished by King Emanuel, whose mother-in-law, Isabella of Spain, threatened to renounce him if he tolerated the enemies of Christ. When, years later, they could settle in Portugal again, they had to wear a yellow hat, by which they were distinguished. Since the eleventh century the governments of Germany, France and Italy found it advisable to assign the Jews certain streets in which they were to live, in order to be secure against the attacks of the mob. These streets were called Jews' quarters, or Ghettos, and were provided with gates, which were shut every evening and opened every morning. (Joseph I., Emperor of Austria, was the first in Germany who permitted the Jews to live outside of the Ghettos.) A second sign of the dark spirit which ruled by-gone ages was the decree which compelled every Jew to wear some degrading badge or peculiar garment by which he was distinguished. Even as late as the time of Frederick William I., King of Prussia (1713 C. E.), the Jews living in his kingdom were obliged to wear green hats. A third and still more oppressive feature was the personal toll. In consideration of certain payments, they could obtain armed escorts to protect their lives and property; this personal toll was levied even when the greater security of the public thoroughfares made an armed escort superfluous. Every Jew wishing to enter a foreign country or the gates of any city was compelled to pay a toll, without which the tax-receiver refused him admission. Not before 1787 was this degrading law repealed, under Joseph II., and done away with in Germany and Austria. In like manner, the Jews' oath, that disgrace to humanity, was abolished in modern days. The cause of all these horrors was by no means the teachings of Christianity, which recommends love to everyone, but the ignorance, coarseness and animal passions of fanatic priests and mobs. Yet there were at all times and in all countries laymen, clergymen, scholars and poets among the Christians who warmly espoused the cause of the Jews and protected them; and Emperor Matthias caused the execution of a baker, Vincenz Fettmilch, who, with his fellows, incited the populace to plunder and massacre the Jews (1400 C. E.).

VII.—THE FRIENDS OF THE JEWS.

Amid all their troubles the Jews had the gratification to know that their friends were always among the best of the land. We shall mention but a few of them:

Charlemagne, who granted them full religious liberty and permitted them to hold public office. He himself employed a Jew in some diplomatic negotiations, and held frequent intercourse with a Jewish merchant.

Louis the Pious created an office, the occupant of which, "Magister Judæorum," was to administer Jewish affairs. Zedekiah, a Jew, was his physician. The weekly markets that were held on the Sabbath he postponed to another day out of deference to the faithful Jews.

Charles the Bald established perfect equality between Jew and Christian.

Henry IV. protected the Jews and punished any who wronged or persecuted them.

Rudolph of Hapsburg even made war on those who falsely accused the Jews of different crimes.

Rudolph II., Maximilian II. and Frederick II. were among the German emperors who showed favor to the Jews.

In Spain there were Alphonso IV., whom Gregory, the Pope, reproached with exalting the "synagogue of Satan above the Church of Christ;" Alphonso VIII. and Alphonso X., who treated the Jews with great distinction; Don Pedro the Cruel was their true friend and protector, his treasurer being one Levy (1537 C. E.), who erected a beautiful synagogue at Toledo.

In Portugal John II. made use of the scientific acquirements of the Jews, when ordering the circumnavigation of Africa.

In Poland Casimir the Great and Sobiesky deserve to be mentioned as friends of the Jews.

In Russia, Peter the Great.

In Sweden, King Christian and his wife.

In Venice they were always treated with justice and impartiality.

In Livorno Ferdinand I. evinced friendliness, and King Roger, in Naples, on his deathbed enjoined his sons to be kind to the Jews, whom he ever had found faithful.

Even some of the great dignitaries of the Church were at times the protectors of the Jews, and popes and bishops not seldom took their part against the mob and some cruel kings; thus Pope Gregory IX., under penalty of excommunication, interdicted Philip II. and Louis the Saint from illtreating the Jews. Innocent IV., in 1244, wrote letters to the bishops of Germany and France, in which he greatly deprecated the injustice done to the Jews, and urgently recommended them to the kindness of both the clergy and the laity; he also censured them for accusing the Jews falsely and holding them accountable for what they never did.

Literary men, too, of high repute and distinction, espoused their cause; for instance: Hugo Grotius, the eminent jurist, Calvin, Wagenseil, Sebastian Munster, Cameron, Ulric, Zchokke, and many others. In like manner the celebrated scholar, John Reuchlin, proved his friendship for the Jews, and when, in 1509, an apostate Jew, by the name of John Pfefferkorn, who was the overseer of the lunatic asylum in Cologne, rose up against Judaism and asserted that if the Talmud should be taken from the Jews they would embrace Christianity, John Reuchlin ably defended the Jews and their literature from the slanderous attacks of the convert, and frustrated his evil designs. Even Martin Luther, the father of the Protestant Reformation, who by no means loved the Jews, turned against their persecutors, and in 1523 wrote on that subject as follows: "Our fools, the Papists, bishops and monks, have hitherto treated the Jews so shamefully that any good Christian might have wished to become a Jew. They have dealt with them as one deals with a dog, not with a human being. They are blood relatives, brothers of our Lord. I, therefore, beg of the Papists, if they are tired of calling me heretic, that they begin to nickname me Jew."

Thus there were at all times noble-minded non-Israelites, who warmly defended the cause of Judaism, and whose humanity and justice entitle them and their memory to Israel's eternal gratitude.

VIII.—JEWISH LIFE AND WORK.

The indescribable sorrows and humiliations of the Jews could but make them appear depressed and cowardly in the eyes of the world. Yet inwardly they retained a stout heart, a clear mind, a love for the divine law, for religious life and science. Strictly virtuous, temperate, modest and unassuming in their mode of living, they found in the family circle and in their domestic relations the highest pleasure and most perfect happiness. They were with very few exceptions excluded from all public offices, trades, agricultural pursuits and possession of real estate; they were compelled to earn a scanty livelihood by small trades, in which they were greatly harrassed; and yet they were contented and happy if, after six days of hard toil, they could spend the Sabbath in the circle of their beloved families, and with the dear ones observe the commands of God. In the house of God, which was at the same time the place of learning (Beth Ham Midrash), the study of the Torah and Talmud was a prominent factor; and while all participated in that study, it was particularly the young who were expected to profit most. Religious training was regarded as one of the most sacred duties devolving upon parents, and there was none, the poorest not excepted, who did not earnestly and sincerely seek to secure for his children (sons or daughters), a thorough and perfect knowledge of the precepts, doctrines and statutes of religion. The rabbis, who were given the title of Morenu (our teacher), stood in high esteem with young and old. They decided in doubtful religious matters, they were the arbiters in all controversies, they instructed, admonished and exhorted the people; they arranged divine service and strongly advocated the fear of God and the purity of morals. Hebrew poets wrote sublime poetical prayers, which were incorporated in the ritual for holy-days, and were known by the name of Piyutim. The manner, custom, habit and mode of devotion, Minhag, differed somewhat, and the Jews were accordingly distinguished as Ashkenazim, *i. e.*, Germans, Polanders, with Austrians, Bohemians, Moravians and Silesians; Sefardim—Portuguese, Spaniards, Italians, etc.

Besides religion, which flourished at this time, science also took a prominent position and high rank. The favorite study of the Jews was medicine, and many Jewish physicians acted in a professional capacity at the courts of famous kings. Thus the celebrated Maimonides was physician to King Salaheddin, of Egypt; Rabbi Meir to the King of Castile; Zedekiah was physician to Louis the Pious, of France, and Elias Montalto to Queen Marie, of Medicis. Some fathers of the Church raised the question as to whether a Jew could be appointed medical adviser of crowned heads; the question was answered in the negative, and yet Pope Boniface XI., Pope Julius III., and others, appointed Jews for their physicians. Of Francis I., in France, it is related that, when once seriously sick, he requested Charles V., Emperor of Germany, to send him a Jewish doctor. The Emperor sent a convert, but Francis refused to accept his services, and said he had plenty of Christian physicians, but needed the assistance of a Jew.

As philosophers, astronomers and mathematicians, the Jews occupied an exalted station. Even eminent and scholarly non-Israelites assert that the Jews in the Middle Ages were the only mediators between the Oriental and Occidental culture. Nor were they less prominent as warriors, and that, notwithstanding their being mostly excluded from military service. In the tenth century they assisted the Christians in driving out of Bohemia the robbers that infested the country, for which the synagogue at Prague was given them as a reward. In the thirteenth century 30,000 Jews were enlisted in the French army. Yet it was reserved for modern times to exhibit their military valor and bravery. Under Napoleon I. many Jews were raised to the ranks of general and Knight of the Legion of Honor. In 1781 the Jewish naval captain, Almeida, fought gallantly against England, and the late wars on this side of the ocean, as well as in Europe, have shown clearly and irrefutably how nobly and bravely the Jews fight for their country, and how many marks of distinction they receive in consequence. Yet their ideal was never war and bloodshed. Peace was what they always loved, as most adapted for the development of the spirit of humanity, of culture and science, as most productive of excellent fruit. Of the many eminent and celebrated men of science who lived in the Middle Ages, we mention:

1. Solomon Ibn Gabirol; 2. Jehuda Halevi; 3. Abraham Ibn Ezra; 4. Maimonides, or Rabbi Moses ben Maimon; 5. Nachmanides; 6. Abarbanel; 7. Rashi; and, 8. Alfasi.

The short biographies of these men follow here.

IX.—SOLOMON IBN GABIROL

Was born at Malaga in the year 1020, and died at Valencia in 1070. He was celebrated and greatly admired as a poet and philosopher. At the age of nineteen he composed a Hebrew grammar in verse. His synagogical songs excel in beautiful language and sublime sentiments. His poetical masterpiece, however, is his " Kether Malchuth " (Crown of Royalty), composed for the glorification of God. This work has been translated into many different languages. Another work from Gabirol's pen, entitled " Fons Vitæ " (Fountain of Life), gives evidence of his clear, incisive and deep reasoning powers, and enjoyed the greatest popularity also in non-Jewish circles. Among Christians, Solomon Ibn Gabirol is known by the name of *Avicenna*. Of the incidents of his life we know very little; of his death, however, the following report is current: There lived an Arabian writer, who greatly envied Gabirol. Unable to put him out of the way, he invited him to his house, murdered and buried him under a fig-tree. That tree ever after bore excellent fruit.

The king, hearing of it, made inquiry of the fortunate possessor of the tree, who eventually confessed his dark deed. The murderer was executed, the remains of the dead poet were exhumed, and, with due honors, buried by the Jews. Short as was his life, he nevertheless accomplished wonders in the field of poetry. The following is a translation of one of his effusions:

" Girt with power, I shall not rest
 Until what I have vowed shall be accomplished.
 Though time shall prove me, like the furnace gold,
 Yet unto wisdom I my allegiance hold.
 Though time refuse me speed and expedition,
 Yet will I dare and do, and not grow cold;
 And with brave heart, with courage undaunted,
 Toil on, persist, until I shall have won.
 Often with fate have I had struggle,
 And, though no conqueror, I neither was the conquered."
—*After Geiger.*

X.—JEHUDA HALEVI,

A man highly celebrated in Israel, even to this day, was born in Toledo in 1086. His poetical effusions are deeply touching, and have been largely incorporated into the prayer-books for Israelites. In his "Zionides," a collection of poems expressive of his warm affection for the Holy Land, which were formerly read on the anniversary of the destruction of Jerusalem (ninth day of Ab), he combines fervor of feeling with sublimity of expression. Heine, the German poet, said of him: "Yes, he was a great poet, a star and torch of his time; his songs a pillar of fire that preceded Israel in the wilderness of his exile." His longings for Jerusalem he expressed in words that seem inspired. A faint idea of them may be conveyed by the following:

"O city of the world, beautiful and majestic,
 For thee I long from distant Western home.
 O that on eagle's wings to the thee I might come nigh,
 That with my tearful face I could but touch thy dust!
 Though kingless, crownless now, yet do I yearn for thee;
 Though serpents vile be now where erst sweet honey flowed,
 O could I kiss thy dust or tread thy ground,
 I'd ask no more; my longing would be stilled."
—*After Sachs.*

Amid greatest dangers he at last undertook a pilgrimage toward that city of the Lord, never more to return to his native Spain. While lost in contemplation of the ruins of the sanctuary, bathed in tears at the sight, he heard not the voice of an Arabian on horseback, and was trampled beneath the hoofs of the fiery steed. Jehuda Halevi, the fervent, polished and accomplished poet, was also a philosopher of great renown. His greatest work is the "Cusari," so called from having for its central figure the King of Chazare, The book, written in the Arabian language, treats of the conversion to Judaism of that prince, Bulan. It is in the form of a dialogue, held by the King of Chazare, first with a Christian, then with a Moslem, and last with a Jew, who, by his logical and rational exposition of the Mosaic faith, won him over to Judaism.

XI.—ABRAHAM IBN EZRA

Was born of very poor parents, in the year 1089. He devoted himself early in life to the acquisition of knowledge. Highly gifted by nature, and working with indefatigable zeal for eminence and celebrity, he succeeded in gaining both. In theology, philosophy, mathematics, medicine, astronomy and languages, he acquired great distinction. In his insatiable thirst for wisdom he undertook many journeys, sought savans, and learned from all. Many writings were the result of his endeavors, part of which he completed in England, and part in Italy. He visited India and Palestine, and wherever the poorly-clad scholar came, he was received with great honors. In one of his travels he came to Jehuda Halevi, whose wealthy, well-educated and highly-aecomplished daughter he obtained in marriage, in a most singular manner. Ibn Ezra, who was then already quite a celebrity, concealed his name and his knowledge from Halevi, whose disciple he was eager to become. Jehuda Halevi accepted him as his pupil, and taught him the rudiments of Jewish lore. One evening the master remained at his study longer than was his wont; the meal was ready, and the household, to which Ibn Ezra also belonged, had waited for him long and in vain. At last he came, and, by way of excusing his tardiness, said that he had been working at a poem, which he was unable to finish. The new scholar looked it over, made some alterations, wrote the conclusion, and, thus complete, handed it back to his master. The rabbi perused it, found it perfect, embraced Ibn Ezra and exclaimed: "You are certainly none other than the celebrated Ibn Ezra; no son-in-law could be more welcome than you are." Soon thereafter the poor young man celebrated his nuptials with the wealthy daughter of Halevi. At the age of seventy-eight, it is said, he died at Rhodes, where he is supposed to be buried.

XII.—MAIMONIDES,

Also called Rabbi Moses ben Maimon, by far surpassed all his contemporaries. No other man has erected for himself so proud and so lasting a monument among the scholars of Israel as this great, profound and original thinker. Maimonides was born in Cordova, on the 14th day of Nissan, 1135. In his earlier years, it is said, he exhibited neither taste nor inclination for study. His father grieved very much at this, and not only severely reprimanded him for his laziness, but locked him up in his room. This had the desired effect. The boy wept, and promised to do better. He traveled on foot to Lucenna, where he enrolled himself as a pupil of Rabbi Joseph ben Meir. This earnest and conscientious teacher took great pains with the promising youth, while he (the boy) was assiduous in his task, working unceasingly, and with the chief object in view of some day affording pleasure to his father, who was ignorant of the whereabouts of his son, and thought he had lost him forever.

After twenty years of hard study, Maimonides returned to Cordova, his native place. But instead of going first to his parental house, he went to the president of the congregation, requesting his permission to occupy the pulpit on the following Sabbath. The news of the arrival of a foreign rabbi spread rapidly through his native city, and curiosity, excitement and expectation were great. The appointed day came. A crowded synagogue greeted the stranger, who had made a favorable impression upon all who had made his acquaintance. The young rabbi began his lecture, the manner and matter of which carried away the multitudes that thronged the sacred edifice. Among the hearers there was also an old, venerable man, who attracted the attention of the rabbi as he left the pulpit. It was the father of Maimonides. The old man, on seeing this young rabbi, bethought himself of his son, whom he supposed dead, and wept, while Maimonides approached the father, whom he recognized, and, embracing him with tearful eyes, said: "I am your son; do you find me unworthy to appear before you?" The overjoyed and highly-elated father pressed him to his heart, took him home, and there he continued his studies with diligence and assiduity; not only of the Talmud, but of Arabian literature, philosophy, medicine, etc. These scientific investigations he successfully strove to harmonize with the principles and doctrines of Judaism, and his celebrated work, "More Nebuchim" (Guide of the Strayed), thoroughly illustrates and systematizes his theories. In the year 1148 the Jews of Cordova were compelled either to renounce their faith and embrace the teachings of Mohammed or to emigrate. Maimonides went to Africa. In the year 1165 he left Fez for Palestine. This trip, made by water, was fraught with many dangers. Arrived in the

Holy Land, he visited all the sacred spots, and set out again for Africa, settled in Fostat, practiced medicine and gained great renown and success in his profession. He also continued his work in the Talmudical science, and the fruit thereof was the Commentary to the Mishna, completed about 1166, in his thirtieth year. After this he wrote the "Yad Hachasaka" (Strong Hand), a code comprising fourteen books, a systematic arrangement of all Talmudical doctrines.

When Turkey extended her dominion over Egypt, Maimonides became acquainted with one of the most prominent generals, through whose influence he was appointed the physician of Sultan Jusup ben Ajub, in Cairo (1201). His enemies, however, accused him of intending to poison the sultan, and he was banished. While in exile he lived in a cave, and devoted himself to the pursuit of scientific studies, the results of which are incorporated in many of his works. Shortly after his banishment, it was found that he had been falsely accused, that he was innocent. The Sultan called him back and reinstated him in his office, which he held to his last day. Though his calling and his official duties required much of his time, he nevertheless worked untiringly in behalf of his people and their science. But, however great, he was frequently attacked, principally on account of his philosophical researches. In Montpelier, his book, *More*, was condemned by the rabbis; he was declared a heretic, and punished with ban and excommunication. This caused considerable disturbance, and eventually resulted in a split between the rabbis of France and Spain. The greatest men, however, were on the side of Maimonides; for example, the well-known grammarian and author of some valuable books, Rabbi David Kimchi. The ban was revoked some time after, and the name of Maimonides was again restored to its former glory.

Maimonides possessed mental powers of the highest degree, and to his profundity of thought there were added and united in him true piety, nobility and love of mankind, which made him beloved and popular with all. So glorified and exalted was he that it was a proverb common in those days: "From Moses (the son of Amram) to Moses (the son of Maimon) there was no man like Moses." He died in the year 1205, and was buried in Tiberias. Jews and Gentiles bewailed his death, and when the sad news had reached Alexandria, seven days later, all the inhabitants of that city were deeply affected at his loss, while the people in Jerusalem, whom the news reached later still, desisted from business and abstained from food as tokens of their mourning. On his tombstone were engraved the words: "Here rests an excellent man."

The thirteen articles of faith which Maimonides wrote contain the summary of the Jewish faith from his standpoint. They are:

1. God is the creator and governor of all beings.

2. God is one; his unity is incomparable. He was, is, and will be.

3. God is incorporeal, and no form can be compared with him.

4. God is the first and the last.

5. God alone is to be worshiped, and none besides him.

6. All the words of the Prophets are truth.

7. The prophecies of Moses are true. He is the first of all Prophets.

8. The Torah which we now possess is the same given to us by Moses.

9. The Torah will never be exchanged for another.

10. God knows all the thoughts and deeds of man.

11. God rewards virtue and punishes vice.

12. A Messiah will arise, though the time be long in coming.

13. God will once revive the dead.

These thirteen articles of faith have in modern times undergone considerable change. Some of them are even entirely discarded.

XIII.—NACHMANIDES (RABBI MOSES BEN NACHMAN, CALLED RAMBAN),

Born in Gerona, Catalonia, in 1195, was likewise one of the eminent men of his time. In early childhood he already acquired a knowledge of Judaism and philosophy; but, unlike Maimonides, was not much devoted to the latter. His preference was for the mystic doctrine, for which reason he was called "Prince of Cabalah." In the year 1263, King Jacob I., of Aragon, invited him to a public discussion with the monk, Paul Christian. Nachmanides came, and in a most spirited, clear and convincing manner he defended his faith, and triumphantly refuted every argument advanced by his opponent. At the age of seventy he was banished from Aragon, and went to Jerusalem. He remained in Palestine until 1270, when he died. Of his works, his Commentary on the Pentateuch, which he completed at an advanced age, deserves mention. Besides this, he wrote several poems, which are a part of the ancient liturgy for New Year's Day, also works on medicine and natural science. He was a famous orator, and highly esteemed for his general knowledge.

XIV.—DON ISAAC ABARBANEL.

Another celebrated Portuguese Hebrew scholar was Don Isaac Abarbanel, born at Lisbon in 1437. His parents, who were very wealthy, traced their genealogy back to David. He enjoyed the advantage of a careful training, and thereby soon gained prominence in the world of letters. His was a profound and versatile mind, by means of which he rose to the exalted position of Privy-Counselor to Alphonso V., King of Portugal. In this position he devoted his attention to politics, commerce and financial management, and performed his tasks with the most scrupulous honesty. When King Alphonso had died, and was succeeded by John II., those envious of Abarbanel accused him before the new king, who readily lent his ear to the calumniations, and pronounced him a conspirator. Warned in time of the danger that threatened his very life, he was forced to flee to Castile, leaving behind him wife, child and property. In his exile he returned to the pursuit of science and continued his Hebrew studies, which consisted mainly of commentaries on different books of the Bible. In Castile he was in the service of Ferdinand and Isabella during eight years. Then came, quite unexpectedly, the famous decree of banishment against the Jews of Spain, at the instigation of Torquemada (see Chap. vi.); and, though the royal pair were willing to make an exception in his case and retain him in their service, he nevertheless resigned the office voluntarily, preferring to share the bitter lot of his brethren. He went to Naples, where, in 1535, twenty-seven years after his death, Benvenida, his daughter-in-law, became the governess of the Grand Duchess of Tuscany. In his new home at Naples he gained the favor of the king, Ferdinand, and of his successor, Alphonso II. When King Charles VIII., of France, attacked Naples, Abarbanel followed his prince, Alphonso, to Messina. After the death of his king he fled to Corfu; then we find him in Apulia, and again in Venice, where he published several treatises. In the year 1508 death overtook the great man, whose life had been so eventful, and who, amid the splendor and pomp of the court, remained true to his people and his faith. His body was conveyed to Padua for sepulture, and the numerous dignitaries, nobles and citizens of Venice, who followed his remains to the grave, manifested their esteem and love for the departed.

XV.—RABBI SOLOMON BEN ISAAC, CALLED RASHI.

The eminent men and scholars hitherto enumerated, inclusive of the celebrated poets, Chasdai· Ibn Shaprut in the tenth and Charisi and Jedajah Bedarshi in the thirteenth century, belong to the Moorish-Spanish school. We shall now turn to the French school, and here we mention as the first and foremost Rabbi Solomon Jizchaki, called Rashi (from the initials of his full name.) He was born in Troyes, France, in 1040, and is the best and most favorably known commentator on the Bible and Talmud. He was a disciple of Rabbenu Gershom, called the "Light of the Exile," who, in a synod convened by him, interdicted polygamy and abrogated forced divorce. Though extremely poor and often in absolute want, Rashi nevertheless made himself acquainted with all the branches of literature then known. Jewish theology, as well as Greek and Arabian literature, found in him their stanch votary. His comments upon the Pentateuch are popular, terse, and therefore easy of comprehension, while his explanations to the Talmud are almost indispensable to its understanding. With all his vast learning, he was so very modest that he seemed ignorant in his own eyes, and ever felt it necessary to increase his stock of knowledge. For this reason he went abroad, and acquired many well-informed and scholarly friends. Traveling in the Orient, he once met a monk. For some time the two conversed and exchanged ideas in a friendly way. But the monk soon began to attack Judaism, which led the two men to dispute and quarrel; they entered their tavern on very bad terms with each other. Suddenly the priest was taken sick, and when Rashi had been informed of the fact, he went to his antagonist's bedside, nursed him with fraternal kindness, and gave him a medicine which soon restored his health. On his recovery, the monk wished to express his thanks to his benefactor, but Rashi said: "You owe me no thanks. Though divided in faith, we must still be united by that love of mankind which Moses enjoined on us. Farewell! And if you meet a suffering Jew, help him as I have helped you." After several years of traveling in foreign lands, he returned home to France, and came to Prague, where he was received by all the Jews with great joy and reverence. Duke Wladislau, under whom the Jews lived, who hated them most bitterly and who embraced every opportunity that offered to manifest his hatred, hearing of the sensation and delight which that strange rabbi had caused his Jewish subjects, had him arrested as a spy. The members of the congregation mourned for Rashi, but he, strengthened by his trust in God and the consciousness of his innocence, retained his calmness and composure. Wladislau was about to utter a sentence of death against Rashi, when the Bishop of Olmutz stepped before the throne of the duke and exclaimed: "In the name of God, I protect and defend this Jew. Not a hair of his head shall be hurt, for he is a man of great learning, of vast knowledge, and is endowed with a noble and generous heart." He thereupon related how, while he was yet a monk, this very Jew had once in the Orient saved his life. The duke, surprised and pleased at this revelation, caused Rashi to be released, and conferred many honors and distinctions upon him. Rashi seized this favorable opportunity, this change of feeling for him, and, prostrating himself before the duke, he implored and secured protection and shelter for the Jews in Prague. Here he married Rebecca, the daughter of the officiating rabbi, Jochanan ben Eliezer.

When Rashi was about to return to his home, in France, with his young wife, he was wounded by the sword of the ducal counselor, Marzerod, who, during the absence of the duke and the archbishop, sought to revenge himself upon the Jews, whom he hated, by killing their favorite. Careful nursing, unremitting watchfulness and constant care on the part of his friends restored him to life and health. His father-in-law, however, concealed this fact, and caused the report to spread that his son-in-law had succumbed under the blow, which had proved fatal, and while his empty coffin was deposited in the grave, Rashi escaped. His life was a wonderful one, and the history thereof is embellished with many legends. Among the remarkable features of his life, which can, however, be described only in the merest outline, there may be mentioned his conversation with Godfred of Bouillion, his vision during a sleepless night, and his invention of the cursory writing. On his journey through Germany he stopped a long time in Worms, where they still show the chair upon which he sat, teaching the word of God. He died on the twenty-ninth day of Tamus, 1105, some sixty-five years of age, in his native place, Troyes. His name, "Chief of Commentators," is mentioned to this day with great respect among the Israelites. His works, which were numerous, exercised a vast influence over Jewish theology, and formed the foundation of the Tosephoth, *i. e.*, explanatory remarks added to the Talmud. The principal works of Rashi are his Commentary on the Bible and the Babylonian Talmud (which was made intelligible and useful only by that commentary) and several treatises, Midrashim, etc. His works and opinions were very praiseworthy. His son-in-law, and especially his two grandsons, Rashbam and Jacob Tom (often mentioned in the Tosephoth, that is, addition to the Talmud), were active in the spirit of their grandfather.

XVI.—ISAAC ALFASI, OR, RABBI ISAAC BEN JOSEPH ALPHES,

Lived in the beginning of the eleventh century. He was born in a small village in the kingdom of Fez, about the year 1013, whence he went to Spain and settled in Seville. He aroused the jealousy of Rabbi Isaac ben Baruch, who was chief of the Academy of Seville. In order to escape the hostility and envy of that man, he left that city in disgust and went to Cordova. But here, too, there was no rest for him, and, finding that he had to suffer much from animosity, he emigrated into Lucena, where he remained until he reached his ninetieth year, when he died. In Lucena peace smiled upon him, and he had the opportunity of following freely his inclinations, which were bent toward study and the practice of charity. His great work, called "Alphasi," which is an extract from and commentary upon the Talmud, received the undivided applause of his contemporaries, and is to this day regarded with the greatest respect. Of his magnanimity and nobility of sentiment, the following may be cited by way of illustration:

Rabbi Isaac ben Baruch, mentioned above, whose hostility had driven Rabbi Alphes from Seville, had a son named Baruch, whom he intended to bring up as a truly religious and well-educated man; but when young Baruch had attained his seventeenth year, his father fell sick, and the hour of his death was fast approaching. On his deathbed he gave his son a letter for Rabbi Alphes, with the order to deliver it in person. The father died, and four weeks later young Baruch came and delivered the letter to Rabbi Alphes. In that letter the former bitter enemy said in substance: " I write this on my deathbed. I sincerely ask your pardon, before I shall be called to my last account. I repent of any wrong committed against you, and in token of my repentance I send you my son, requesting you to educate and to instruct him in your spirit, that some day he may become like you. Will you grant the request of a dying man?" Alphes was touched, and, embracing the youth, said: "You are not entirely fatherless; from this day I consider you as my son." Rabbi Alphes educated his charge with great care and love; and, thanks to his generous foster-father, Baruch became an eminent man.

XVII.—SEVERAL CELEBRITIES IN GERMANY.

Rabbi Amnon, of Mayence, lived in the thirteenth century in the city from which he took his surname. He was a man universally respected, both for his piety and learning. The elector of the Palatinate of Mayence was his friend, and conferred upon him many distinctions. But the courtiers could not brook that a Jew should thus enjoy princely favor, and they, therefore, intrigued against the pious man by persuading the prince to convert the rabbi to Christianity. Their plot succeeded. The prince used all his eloquence, but in vain. He then requested him to appear in his closet, where he spoke to him thus: "You know, Amnon, how I love you; do me the favor to become a Christian." But Amnon replied: "I duly appreciate thy consideration, my lord and master, and I am ready to shed every drop of my blood for you, but I can not under any circumstances become guilty of hypocrisy and perjury. If I change my God to-day, might I not to-morrow become faithless to my sovereign?" When he was still further and closer pressed, he begged for time to reflect. Three days were granted him, but he had hardly left the palace before he bitterly reproached himself for his wavering—for having entertained for a single moment, however remotely, the idea of becoming faithless to his God. Disconsolate because of that hasty utterance, which to him appeared equivalent to a promise, he wept and mourned, and fasted for three days. The respite granted him had elapsed, but he remained at home. He was summoned, but he disobeyed the summons three times. At last the prince had recourse to violence, and had him brought by force. "Why did you not keep your word, Amnon?" the prince harshly asked the poor man, who by the self-imposed affliction had grown so weak as to present a most pitiable aspect; "are you willing to become a Christian?" "No," calmly replied Amnon; "and I have not come because I could not comply with your wish. But I am ready to suffer, nay, I am willing to pronounce upon myself, if you will permit it, this sentence: The tongue that has indulged in hypocrisy—that has lied—may be cut out." "No," replied the prince, "the feet that refused to come hither shall be cut off and your whole body shall be chastised." The sentence was carried into effect; the order was promptly executed. The mutilated martyr, who had never uttered a sound of complaint, was at last carried to his house, and even there he endeavored to console his sorrowing family by persuading them that he fully deserved the severe visitation. The New Year's Day, Rosh Hashana, being celebrated a few days later, he ordered himself and his severed limbs to be carried to the synagogue, and the litter was placed near the reader's desk. Before this official wanted to pronounce the "thrice holy" in the Kedusha, Rabbi Amnon called out: "Hold, let me sanctify the name of God!" and with an affecting voice he exclaimed: "Let us glorify our Lord, for thou, O Eternal, art our king." After having spoken these words he began to recite a prayer which he had composed, beginning with the words, ונתנה תוקף (Let us describe the sublimity of the Day of Judgment.) The reader then continued, and when he had uttered the words, "He is our God, there is no other," Amnon interrupted him once more and exclaimed in a loud voice: אמת (that is the truth), and expired. His teacher, Kalonymos, who had remembered every word of that impressive prayer of the martyr, sent copies of the same to every Jewish congregation, and by them it was incorporated into the liturgy for the New Year's Day and the Day of Atonement, and to this day is recited on those days after the Kedusha in the Mussaph prayer.

Among the German rabbins we will also mention Rabbi Meir ben Baruch, better known by the name of Maharam of Rothenberg, who, while seeking safety by flight, was caught by the Bishop of Basel and thrown into a dungeon. From this imprisonment his faithful and celebrated disciple, Asher ben Jechiel, also called Rosh, sought to liberate him; but the ransom demanded was too great, and after Asher ben Jechiel had spent his whole fortune in fruitless endeavors to secure the freedom of his beloved master, Maharam died, in 1293. The son of Rosh, Jacob, wrote the Turim, a casuistical work in four books or volumes, the basis of the Shulchan Aruch, the author of which was Rabbi Joseph Karo, of Zephath (1488-1575). The Shulchan Aruch is divided into four parts, viz.: Eben Haezer, treating of marital laws; Choshen Mishpat, of legal cases; Yoreh Deah, of ritual laws; and Orach Chayim, of Sabbath, festival and other ceremonies. Rabbi Moses Iserles, of Cracow, also called Rema, from the initials of his name, enlarged the Schulchan Aruch by copious notes; the same did Joseph Albo, who acquired considerable fame and celebrity as a religio-philosophic writer, through his work, Ik Karim, *i. e.*, principles of faith.

We must not forget the great poet, Emanuel ben Solomon, who lived at Rome in the thirteenth century, and who wrote some love songs, rare products of Jewish literature, which were much admired by the Gentiles. He also wrote an excellent commentary on the books of Job, Psalms, Proverbs and others, for which he was greatly applauded. Another Italian scholar of renown was Elias Levita, of Padua, the author of an excellent Hebrew grammar, which is admired to this day.

XVIII.—MYSTICISM, CABALAH.

The study of the Tora and the Talmud was no more the exclusive occupation of scholars and laymen. In the minds of most of them superstition had taken root, and this led them to occupy their time with a sort of mystic science, which, owing to its being traditional, was called Cabalah. The object of this study was the interpretation of visions, dreams, good and evil spirits, migration of the soul (Gilgul), etc. The oldest cabalistic work, which was already known by the Gaonim, is the book "Yezirah," creation. In the thirteenth century Moses de Leon issued the Sohar, which contains the fundamental doctrines of this mysticism. Many who occupied their time with the study of Cabalah professed to be performers of miracles; thus, Rabbi Isaac Luria, whose disciples spread the belief that by means of this science wonders could be performed. But the Cabalah has also many opponents, such as Elias del Medigo and Rabbi Jehudah Modena; yet for a time the Cabalists prospered and found credence in their most absurd and extravagant claims. They were even regarded as Messiahs, though only for a short time. Soon, however, the more sober and less infatuated discovered how those cabalists strayed from the right way.

Sabbathai Zevi, one of the prominent representatives of that class of deceived deceivers, was born at Smyrna in 1625. Of all the Cabalists, pseudo-Messiahs and deluded pretenders, none was more contemptible or more cunning, and none more remarkable than Sabbathai Zevi. His father dealt in poultry, and the young and highly gifted son directed his attention to the study of that mysterious science, the Cabalah, and publicly discussed its advantage at the age of eighteen.

Though at first he was laughed at, he soon succeeded in gaining a large number of followers, who respected and revered him as a saint. His fame spread far and wide, and very soon he was recognized, not only in all Turkey, but even in foreign parts, as the divinely-sent Messiah. From Holland, Poland and Italy, his admirers came to pay him homage, to make him costly presents and to pray for his life. During his lectures, his hearers and disciples sat at his feet, wrapped in Talith and Tephilim, fasted, prayed, and practiced abstinence. Some enlightened men, faithful believers in God, denounced him as a false Messiah and as a vile deceiver, but the masses, naturally credulous, and often "making the wish father to the thought," clung to him, and trusted his solemn promises and deceptive hopes, and awaited patiently yet confidently to be led back to Palestine by him, and to see him, as a scion of the house of David, occupy the regal throne of his illustrious ancestor. Like every other Messiah before him, he appointed a forerunner, a man by the name of Nathan Benjamin, who was to announce the coming of the Messiah. Nathan Benjamin, the representative of Elijah the Prophet, sent letters to all countries, the purport of which was that the Messiah had come, and would soon assume the diadem; that he would then disappear for a time, and come back again accompanied by Moses, and thereupon the restoration to Palestine would be set on foot. He would enter the holy city on a lion, which was to come down from heaven, and whose tongue was to be like a seven-headed serpent. By the breath of his mouth he would kill thousands of his enemies, and in Jerusalem he would descend from heaven, offer sacrifices, restore the dead to life, and perform other miracles too numerous to mention. While in Jerusalem, Zevi was opposed by some and upheld by others in his claims; but pending negotiations he went to Egypt to espouse a bride, who, as he averred, had been sent from heaven. He returned with the daughter of a Polish rabbi, who had been reared by Gentiles. This was Zevi's third marriage, but it was a farce, as had been his marriages previously contracted. His opponents resisted a public ceremony, and some rabbis pronounced the sentence of death upon him, declaring him and his accomplice to be impostors, none of whom had any qualifications for the position which they claimed. Zevi escaped and went to Smyrna, where, after living four years in seclusion, he arose again, and found the magic of his name unimpaired. But when he arrived at Constantinople Sultan Mohammed IV., who heard of his agitations, denounced him as a disturber of the peace and caused his arrest. But even during his imprisonment for two years his followers still paid him homage. A Polish scholar, Nehemiah by name, visited Zevi, recognized the vile impostor, and, having established his identity beyond any doubt, he went to Adrianople, where he informed the authorities of the true character of the pretender. The courts thereupon proposed to test his Messiahship, and offered him the choice between allowing himself to be pierced through and embracing Islamism. Zevi chose the latter, but still persisted in acting the part of the redeemer. Ten years after this change of his religion, he was carried, at the instigation of his enemies, into Bosnia, where he died, in Belgrade, in 1673.

Other similar cabalistic parties arose in later times.

Israel Baal Shem Tobh (man of good name or repute), also known as Besht, from the initials of his name, established the sect of Beshts, or Chassidim; and Joseph Frank, the Frankists.

XIX.—BENEDICT SPINOZA—GABRIEL OR URIEL ACOSTA.

Baruch or Benedict Spinoza, born at Amsterdam in the year 1632, of highly respected Portuguese parents, was an eminent Jewish theologian, who reached the highest point of philosophical scholarship in Israel. Indeed, philosophy became the element of his life; to it he devoted all his time, and the study thereof so engrossed his mind that he neglected the religion in which he had been born, and became estranged from the synagogue. The rabbis demanded of him a strict observance of the religious ceremonies, but this he positively refused. The consequence was that he was excommunicated. Spinoza heeded it not, but persevered in his course, which exposed him to numerous persecutions. One man, a fanatic, deeming the death of such a man as Spinoza beneficial to Judaism, waylaid him, with the intention of assassinating him; but Spinoza warded off the blow and saved his life, only his coat being pierced by the dagger. That coat he sacredly preserved as a memorial of the event. But, although Spinoza had formally broken with all ceremonialism, he never renounced his faith, although tempting offers were made to him to embrace Catholicism. He suffered want and privation, and in his greatest poverty he became a glass-cutter, by which occupation he earned a scanty livelihood. He never accepted any presents, and when they were offered him he refused them, gently but firmly.

In conversation he was always calm, friendly, affable and patient. When his day's work—scientific researches and the arduous labor of writing and the preparation of physical instruments, microscopes and telescopes — was done, he delighted in light diversions, and found even the war among spiders sufficiently interesting. Of his great spiritual powers he has left abundant proofs, and his philosophical system is even to this day an object of earnest study and of profound admiration. Charles Louis, the Elector of the Palatinate, offered him the chair of Philosophy at the University in Heidelberg. Spinoza, however, declined the proffered honor, because he could not reconcile his liberal views and privilege of liberty of teaching with the reigning religion, which, according to the policy of the elector, he was not permitted to interfere with. He died in the prime of life, only forty-five years of age, leaving behind him a spotless name, an unsullied character, and a well-merited reputation for spiritual greatness, which even his adversaries were forced to acknowledge and to praise. To modern times it was reserved to fully understand him, and his name is now uttered with reverence, while his fame and memory have recently been perpetuated by a monument that was erected in 1877.

As in olden times, Elisha ben Abuya had gone astray in consequence of his indulgence in hypothetical speculations, thereby becoming first a skeptic and then a renegade to the pure Israelitish doctrine, so it was with Gabriel (Uriel) Acosta, a learned Portuguese. Accompanied by his mother and brother, he went to Amsterdam, where he returned to the religion of his Jewish ancestors. But Judaism, being then more Rabbinism than the pure Mosaism he had expected to find, caused grave doubts to rise within him. He consequently attacked and violated the Mosaic faith, for which he was excommunicated and bitterly persecuted by the rabbis of Holland. In his misery he requested his worst enemy to shoot him, and, when the bullet failed, he committed suicide. His works, too, betoken great knowledge and mental acumen, but because of his speculative and skeptical propensities he did not properly utilize his mental faculties.

XX.—MANASSE BEN ISRAEL.

In the night of the Middle Ages, Holland had become the asylum and the friendly home of the Jews. And England was to imitate Holland's noble example in the middle of the seventeenth century. Manasse ben Israel, a prominent scholar and preacher at Amsterdam (born in 1609, at Lisbon), addressed a petition to Cromwell, then Dictator of England, to grant the Jews permission to settle in that island. Cromwell submitted the petition to Parliament, with the strong recommendation to grant it, but the British clergy, spreading hostile letters, articles and pamphlets, prevented the prompt passage of the bill. Then Manasse indited a reply to those fanatical heads of the Church, and in that defensive article, entitled " Salvation of the Jews," he succeeded, by a thorough refutation of those malicious charges, in showing the unjustness of the suspicion, and, by thoroughly and irrefutably exposing the prejudices, in gaining his point, and securing for his brethren the right of settlement in England. Great Britain, which had been for 300 years inaccessible to the Jews, now opened her gates, and many took up their habitation there and soon gained the love and respect of their new fellow-citizens. Manasse ben Israel was the author of numerous theological, philosophical and other writings, which were highly appreciated, even among Christians, of whom some celebrities, as, for instance, Hugo Grotius, were his friends. Manasse was a poor man, and Cromwell granted him a pension for life of 100 pounds annually.

Returning to Holland from England, he died, in 1657, deeply mourned by his brethren in the faith, as well as by his contemporaries.

Part III.

MODERN TIMES.

I.—THE EMANCIPATION OF THE JEWS IN FRANCE.

The French Revolution in 1789 marked a general improvement in the condition of the Israelites. The scales fell from the eyes of the mighty rulers, they became aware of their injustice, and in most countries they began to emancipate their Jewish subjects, *i. e.*, to place them on equal terms with those of other creeds and doctrines. France led her sister States in this work of liberation, and the oppressed and downtrodden Israelites began to feel the dawning of a brighter era for them in that country. In the year 1791 the Jews were granted the same rights and privileges which the other inhabitants and citizens of France enjoyed.

When Napoleon ascended the throne, and several complaints were made to him against the Alsatian Jews, he assembled a convention, consisting of 100 of the most prominent Jews (1806). In this meeting they were afforded the opportunity to refute the charges brought against them, and to remove all causes for complaints. The object was gained, and those 100 representative men, forming the deputation, led and headed by the celebrated Abraham Furtado, of Bordeaux, succeeded in triumphantly clearing themselves and their brethren. Twelve grave questions were asked, among them their opinion of the authority of the State, intermarriage between Jews and Gentiles, etc. The answers were highly satisfactory to the Emperor, who desired the establishment of a Synhedrin, consisting, like the old one, of seventy-one members. This body of men was to decide in matters religious and social, and their decisions were to find public recognition. This was done, causing joy and gratification to the Israelites. But though the decree of emancipation had gone forth and had been incorporated in the statute-book, it was only in 1830, during the July Revolution, that the principle of equality was recognized in all circles of the French populace, and that the Jewish consistory was established and the rabbinical school at Metz subventioned by the State. During the debates on a new constitution, the distinction previously existing between Jews and Christians was done away with, and the resolution carried directing that the salaries of Jewish rabbis, as well as those of Christian clergymen, should be paid out of the royal treasury. Israelites attained to honor and distinction; they filled offices of trust, and proved themselves eminently worthy of the confidence reposed in them. In that year, 1830, there were chosen from among the Israelites a lieutenant-general, army and navy officers, public physicians, professors of universities, lawyers, notaries, etc. And this happy turn in their external affairs neither estranged them from their faith nor prompted them to become callous and indifferent to the sad condition of their brethren elsewhere. It rather incited them to use their power and influence for the abolition of any oppressive law affecting them. In 1840 there was living in Damascus a monk of the Capuchin Order, who for two years had studied medicine. One day the monk was found dead, evidently the victim of foul play. It was asserted that when last alive he had been seen in the Jews' quarter. Suspicion at once rested upon the Jews, who were promptly charged with the murderous deed. Excitement ran high. The mob became furious. The most prominent Jews of Damascus were tortured, or cast into dungeons. All Europe was filled with consternation. In this critical time the French and English Jews resolved to send a deputation to Damascus, to take proper measures to quell the disturbance and to shield and defend their unfortunate brethren, Two celebrated men, Isaac Adolphe Cremieux (who died February 10, 1880), of Paris, and Moses Montefiore, of London, repaired to the scene of trouble, for the purpose of bringing the matter before a competent tribunal. They obtained access to the Sultan, before whom they pleaded the case of their incarcerated brethren, and secured not only their liberation but a public declaration of their innocence. There are about 48,000 Jews in France.

II.—THE JEWS IN HOLLAND AND BELGIUM.

From France the emancipation of the Jews spread and took root in Holland and Belgium. On the 12th of September, 1798, a declaration for the full grant of liberty to the Jews was promulgated in Holland; and from that day they have been citizens in the full sense of the word. Holland has now about 75,000 Jews, partly of German and partly of Portuguese extraction. In Amsterdam alone there are about 25,000.

In Belgium, which became independent of Holland in 1831, the Jews were granted full enjoyment of all civil rights. Their position has remained favorable. They are distinguished in the army, among the men of science, and in commerce. Belgium has a Jewish population of about 2,000.

III.—THE JEWS IN GERMANY.

Germany followed the example of her sister States, and became tolerant toward the Jews. As early as 1781, Professor Dohm, an author of great renown, advocated the cause of the Israelites, and warmly and forcibly defended their rights as men and as citizens. But his earnest efforts, as well as those of others, such as Lessing, Krug and others, did not avail much. The Jews continued in their subordinate positions, and even the disgraceful personal toll was kept intact. Not until the Kingdom of Westphalia was established by Napoleon I. did their lot become a more favorable one. First in Westphalia, then in Baden, Hamburg, Bremen, Lubeck, Mecklenburg and Prussia. But even then the old prejudices and persecutions did not entirely cease, and it frequently seemed to them as though the specters of the Middle Ages had risen from their tombs. In Frankfort, Wurzburg and in other cities it was a quite frequent occurrence that the Jews were pursued by the mob, shouting: "Hep! Hep!" (the initials of "Hierosolyma est perdita," *i. e.*, Jerusalem is lost.) Often, too, they were threatened with banishment, or scorned and maligned with expressions, or in pamphlets, breathing the bitterest hatred. In short, their position was by no means an enviable one. To Gabriel Rieser, of Hamburg (1806–1863), the peerless champion and bold defender of the Jewish faith and name, it was reserved to secure the emancipation of his brethren. His inspired and zealous work and his earnest plea for the recognition of their rights as human beings, was at last successful, after many futile attempts made by others.

Frederick the Great and, after him, Frederick William II., were two monarchs filled with the earnest desire to politically improve the condition of their Jewish subjects; but the various troubles with other countries claimed their attention, and the question of the emancipation of the Jews remained in abeyance. But however well disposed Frederick the Great and his successors were, and however zealously the immortal Gabriel Rieser fought for the rights of his brethren, the epoch of Israel's liberty was due to and prepared by the glorious exertions of another great man, of whom we shall speak in the succeeding chapter. He it was who rose like a sun of salvation, with healing in his wings, over Germany's darkening horizon, who paved the way for freedom, for toleration and humanity, not only in Germany, but in other countries as well. This man, justly revered by the Israelites of modern times, occupying a prominent niche in the Temple of fame,—this man, who has secured for himself a name in the literature of Germany, and who has left behind him an imperishable monument, was Moses Mendelssohn.

IV.—MOSES MENDELSSOHN,

The son of poor parents, was born at Dessau, September 6, 1729. His first instruction he received from Rabbi David Frankl, in Dessau. At the age of ten the boy had acquired a respectable knowledge of Jewish lore. With great diligence he next applied himself to the study of the philosophical works of Maimonides. In his anxiety to learn, and eagerness for mental progress, he worked so untiringly that his health became impaired and his body deformed. Rabbi David Frankl subsequently moved from Dessau to Berlin, and thither young Mendelssohn followed him. Fighting the wolf of hunger that often approached the young student, suffering want and privation otherwise, he found in Rabbi David Frankl not only a teacher, but a warm-hearted friend. Through the influence of this man Moses obtained free board (receiving his meals in different families on different days) and lodging; and, by copying the works of his teacher, the poor, struggling student earned a little money, wherewith he supplied all his wants. He next turned his attention to the study of the German language, which was then not universally known by the Jews, who spoke the corrupt mixture of German and Hebrew, and soon thoroughly mastered it. He read the German classics with great avidity, studied mathematics with Israel Samosz, a man whom he had befriended, and the old classics with the assistance of the physician, Mr. Kish. The English and French languages he also added to his curriculum. Soon his financial condition improved. The Jewish physician, Gomperz, recommended him to Mr. Bernhard, a manufacturer of silk, who employed him as private tutor to his children (1750). Through Dr. Gomperz he also made the acquaintance of Gotthold Ephraim Lessing, the celebrated German author, who was fond of playing chess, and to whom Moses was recommended as a good player. Their acquaintance soon ripened into the most intimate and enduring friendship. Lessing and Mendelssohn, as they were devoted to each other during their entire lives, live to this day united in the memory of posterity, and the name of the one involuntarily suggests the other. Mendelssohn once received from his friend an English book, and when he asked him how he liked it, the answer of Mendelssohn was: "I could produce such a thing myself." A few weeks later Mendelssohn showed Lessing one of his own manuscripts for perusal, and, without the knowledge of its author, Lessing had it printed. It was "Mendelssohn's Philosophical Conversations." Printed copy in hand, the stanch friend of Moses Mendelssohn entered the latter's house and handed him the book, which the author at once and to his great surprise recognized as his own. That book created a profound sensation, and from that time Moses of Dessau became a celebrity. Bernhard made him partner of his business, and in 1762 Mendelssohn married the well-educated Frummet Guggenheim, of Hamburg. They had four sons and four daughters. (Felix Mendelssohn Bartholdy, the celebrated composer, was a grandson of Moses Mendelssohn.)

About this time the Jewish religion was made an object of attack by the enemies of the Bible, who claimed that Judaism did not teach the immortality of the soul. In vindication of his faith, and still more as a rebuke to his antagonists, Moses published his " Phaedon," in which he demonstrated that second principle doctrine of his religion. This work, too, met with abundant success, and through it he became world-renowned. Many celebrities and acknowledged lights of science sought to gain his friendship, for he was a man whose versatile talent and deep knowledge were coupled with modesty and affability. He was elected a member of the Academy at Berlin, which learned body had unanimously awarded him the prize in 1784; Frederick II., however, had refused his consent to its presentation. On hearing of the decision of the king, which was adverse to his election, Mendelssohn, with great equanimity, remarked: "It is much better and more honorable to be found worthy of an academical chair by the Academy, and not by the king, than to become a member of the Academy by the king's word, over the will and the decision of the academicians." Mendelssohn was a noble, pious Jew, thoroughly imbued with the doctrines of his religion. The mental improvement of his Jewish brethren was the object which he had mostly at heart, and he earnestly strove for their social elevation.

Lavater, a celebrated clergyman of Zurich, greatly respected Mendelssohn, but sought to convert him to his faith. The great man gently and spiritedly repelled all these attempts, and by his fine tact and elegance of speech he succeeded in preventing attacks upon and all prejudices against Judaism.

His translation of the Bible into German marked an important epoch in the history of Judaism, affecting not only the Jews in Germany, but even those in foreign countries. This translation not only facilitated the understanding of the sacred book, but it was also a means of teaching the German language to his brethren. Yet he did not escape the animosity of many, who offered strenuous objection to the before unheard-of innovation, and who finally caused his excommunication. Nevertheless, the Bible spread rapidly, and found access into many, many houses. In honor of his dearest friend, Lessing, he published his "Morning Hours," spirited and profound conversations about God and the influence of religion upon human society. These conversations had in reality been held between himself and his children or friends. This work had the effect of securing for him the name of the "German Plato." In his work called "Jerusalem," he treats with much erudition the principles of spiritual liberty, of freedom of conscience and faith. He was the third Moses in Israel's history — a man of God, uniting within himself religion and science in a manner rarely found in any one individual, and setting a noble example to his people and to mankind. The better social position which the Jews occupied during the years from 1850 to 1870 —their social and political equality, guaranteed them by the Constitution—is due to the exertions of Moses Mendelssohn, who during his lifetime prepared and paved the way for progressive ideas, and laid the foundation for the proud temple of tolerance and liberty.

The fourth day of January, 1786, is justly marked as a day of gloom for Israel, for on it Moses Mendelssohn — the man, the Israelite, the scholar, the friend and the great reformer—departed this life. His remains were followed to their last resting-place by a vast concourse of warm friends and admirers.

His memory is immortal. He has carved for himself a proud monument, which is adorned with the chaplets: "The elevation of Israel, the ennoblement of the German language and science, his generous character and his philosophical works." (In 1879, the 150th anniversary of Mendelssohn's birth, and also that of Lessing, were worthily celebrated in Germany by the publication of a magnificently executed "Lessing-Mendelssohn Gedenkbuch," a memorial volume. Besides this, the united German Israelitish congregations, "Gemeindebund," purchased the house in Dessau in which Mendelssohn was born, and dedicated it as the home of poor Israelitish scholars; the family of Mendelssohn, now living in Berlin, contributing toward the purchase of that house.) In many German cities there were also established "Mendelssohn societies," for the promotion of Jewish lore and science.

Of the friends and disciples of Mendelssohn there may be mentioned:

1. The non-Israelitish poet, Lessing, whose masterpiece is that sublime drama, "Nathan the Wise." In this inspired production, the poet glorifies Judaism, teaches tolerance toward those of other creeds, and "Nathan," the most prominent and central figure of that drama, is the faithful portrait of Mendelssohn.

2. Hartwig Wessely, born in Hamburg in 1722 and died in Hamburg in 1805. He was a talented and imaginative author, who systematically attacked and persistently fought against sanctimoniousness and ignorance; he was distinguished also as a poet, orator, theologian and grammarian.

3. Herz Homberg, the tutor of Mendelssohn's children, and celebrated for his improvement in the Jewish school system in Galicia.

4. Isaac Euchel, the first translator of liturgical prayers.

After Mendelssohn there worked in his spirit David Friedlander, alderman in Berlin; Bensev; Dubno; the poet Ephraim Kuh; the philosopher Dr. Marcus Herz; Professor Levisohn, and many others.

V.—THE JEWS IN AUSTRIA.

No prince had ever been kindlier disposed toward the Jews than Emperor Joseph II. In 1782 he promulgated the well-known "Edict of Toleration," by which the Jews were guaranteed full recognition of their inalienable rights; they were not to be excluded from any advancement; the public schools were to be opened to them, and the acquisition of knowledge of German made easy. They were also to be admitted into military service, to have the privilege of establishing factories and engaging in agricultural pursuits, with the restriction, however that they should employ only Hebrew laborers, in order to attract many to that occupation. His successors while not positively antagonistic, were lukewarm in matters concerning the Jews, and while the emancipation did not retrograde, its progress was very slow indeed. Full emancipation of the Jews in Austria is comparatively of recent date. With the accession to the throne of Francis Joseph I., the present emperor, in 1848, all possible rights and privileges were granted them. Previous to that year, however, they were repeatedly harassed and confined; thus, for instance, the Jews in Galicia were not permitted to follow a profession, while in their small trades they were greatly taxed; thus, in Bohemia and Moravia only the eldest or first son of any family could obtain permission from the government to marry; the Jew was permitted to acquire land, but was compelled to work it himself. In Hungary the Jews gained more and more liberties and privileges. In 1844 they were allowed to engage in art or science, to study and practice law, become pharmacists and engineers or acquire landed property. About the year 1864,

Baron Eotvos, the liberal, learned and tolerant Minister of the Interior, convened an Israelitish Congress to arrange several matters affecting Jewish life, and to deliberate on the best way for employing the school fund of 1,000,000 guilders, which the king had placed at the disposal of those who desired the establishment of better schools and the employment of better teachers.

VI.— THE CONDITION OF THE JEWS IN OTHER EUROPEAN STATES.

The Jews in Russia were most unfortunately situated. In July, 1768, Empress Catherine issued a manifesto, which breathed hatred and destruction against Poland and the Jews. Alexander I., to whom the Jews had rendered valuable services in the wars of 1812, found no time to consider their condition. He acknowledged, it is true, his indebtedness to them, and promised to ameliorate their condition, but besides these and other negative advantages, they gained nothing. When, in 1825, however, his successor, Nicholas I., ascended the throne, he at once instituted a systematic and unparalleled persecution of his Jewish subjects. In the year following his accession to the throne, he banished the Jews from St. Petersburg and Moscow; in 1828 he compelled them to enter military service, but without any prospect of promotion. The most proscriptive laws were enacted, which embittered the lives of the Jews; and not until Alexander II. (recently assassinated in St. Petersburg) became Czar did their condition change for the better, although even now, at this writing, they justly complain of great misery and oppression at the hands of the populace, which the government seems unable to control.

Most of the Russian (Polish) Jews keep aloof from their non-Jewish fellow-citizens, preserve a peculiarity of dress, use a corrupt German in conversation, and by their singular intonation of words and by many repulsive habits they have exposed themselves to the ridicule of others. The Russian Jews, however, justly boast of many bright and well-informed men, who diligently pursue the study of religion, the Talmud and profane science; many among them are mechanics and agriculturists, while others delight in indolence, and thereby throw themselves into the arms of poverty. Since the accession to the Russian throne of Alexander II., their social and political condition has somewhat improved. The number of Jews living in Russia is decidedly greater than that to be found in any other country.

Infinitely better situated in every respect are the Jews in England. The seed sown by Manasse ben Israel (see above, Part II., Chap. xx.,) has borne magnificent fruit. By great diligence, virtue and charity they proved themselves eminently worthy of their liberty, while through these very agencies they acquired power, gained wealth and secured influence. As early as 1856 David Solomons was elected Lord Mayor of London, while to-day many Jews occupy positions of trust and honor. It is unnecessary to enumerate the many who are distinguished by the government, but we can not omit to make mention of the most illustrious and prominent British Jew of this century — the man who has lived a long and useful life, who has ever espoused and even now espouses the cause of his brethren; the man to whom all Israelites owe so much for his untiring energy and zeal on their behalf—Sir Moses Montefiore, now ninety-six years of age.

In Switzerland, too, the condition of the Jews has much improved. In the fifteenth century they were restricted to the Canton Aargau, and there they were permitted to live only in Lingenau and Endigen. Even in the eighteenth century they were not allowed to bury their dead upon their native soil, but on an island near by, called "Jew Island." With the dawn of the present century, however, these restrictions were gradually removed. The 10,000 Jews who now inhabit Switzerland enjoy full liberty and equal rights with the other inhabitants. Some twenty-five years ago there was an attempt made by the government to abolish the Shechita (that is, the killing of beasts according to the rabbinical code). It was held to be barbarous and cruelty to animals. But the energetic interference of the learned rabbi, Dr. Kayserling, frustrated the attempt. He adduced, in addition to his own arguments, the testimony of renowned non-Jewish scholars, who unanimously testified that the rabbinical Shechita was the easiest and most painless manner of killing animals.

When Victor Emanuel adopted the Constitution, by a provision of which the temporal power of the Pope ceased, the Jews of Italy, and of her capital, Rome, began to hear the rustling of the wings of a new and better era. The restrictive measures concerning the Jews, which had proved fatal to the free and full development of Judaism, were removed, and at once the morning dawned, after a long, dark and dreary night. While yet under Austrian rule, there was established a celebrated rabbinical seminary at Padua, at which, among other notabilities, the eminent scholar, S. D. Luzzato, was one of the professors. This seat of learning ceased to exist when Lombardy and Venice passed into the power of Italy.

The Jews of Italy of the present day excel in industrial and agricultural pursuits. In 1858 an event transpired which deserves to be mentioned here. There lived in Rome at that time a Jewish family by the name of Mortara. They had a very bright and promising boy, who, by order of the Pope, was forcibly taken from his parents, baptized and educated in the Catholic Church. A cry of indignation rose, the Jews all over the earth loudly protested against this highhanded outrage, and Sir Moses Montefiore went to Rome in order to secure from the Pope the return of that boy, but in vain. The helplessness of the Jews led them to form a union for the more effectual protection of their rights, and in 1860, with Adolphe Cremieux as the head, the "Alliance Israelite Universelle" was formed, which has since done a great amount of good toward securing and defending the rights of the Jews.

Step by step the Jews progressed toward liberty; country after country joined the proud ranks of enlightenment, justice and humanity. Thus the year 1838 signalized the marked improvement of the condition of the Jews in Turkey. After the Russo-Turkish War (1853-56), Sultan Abdul Medjid placed them on full equality with his Mussulman subjects, and his successor, Abdul Aziz (murdered in 1876), imposed upon them equal duties and granted them equal rights with the other citizens.

The Jews all over the European continent, recognizing the good intentions of the Turkish government, endeavored to do their share toward making their co-religionists in the East worthy of the grace of their ruler. They established schools and other institutions at Jerusalem, Cairo and Constantinople, and the Rothschilds, Moses Montefiore, and the native Americans, Juda Touro and Simmons, bore the expenses of erecting and maintaining those institutions.

Most of the Jews of Turkey, however, are very poor, and depend largely on the support of the charitably inclined. In the last Russo-Turkish war, where many of the unfortunate Jews were compelled to flee, their European brethren, the "Alliance Israelite" (mentioned before and to be spoken of in a later chapter), and especially one of their co-religionists, Baron Hirsch—who gave 1,000,000 francs for their support— clearly manifested their charitable disposition and their magnanimity. Greece, Servia, Roumania and Bulgaria, formerly under Turkish vassalage, offered obstinate resistance to the recognition of the rights of the Jews. With the exception of Greece those small principalities were, and to some extent are yet, the very hot-beds of intolerance, persecution and oppression. Until very recently they were regarded and treated as aliens; though they had sacrificed their property and spilt their blood for their country, they were excluded from public office and rank, they could acquire no landed property; even in commerce, or the renting of taverns or mechanical pursuits, they met with serious and vexatious opposition, and nowhere did the Jews of the present decade suffer so much and such cruel maltreatment as in Roumania and Bulgaria. Murder, plunder and expulsion, rape and extermination were the watchwords of the mob, and the government did nothing, and now does very little, for the oppressed. In 1878 there met a congress at Berlin, representing all European governments, and then and there, under the presidency of Prince Bismarck, one of the greatest diplomats of this age, the recognition of the independence of these States was agreed upon, on condition that they would grant equal rights to all, irrespective of their faith or creed. The late Benjamin Disraeli, Earl of Beaconsfield, who died in 1881, played a prominent part at that congress. Although these conditions are not yet fully complied with, it is to be hoped that in due time the barriers will fall, and men will be judged by their deeds and not by their creeds.

VII.—THE JEWS IN ASIA.

Palestine, the Holy Land, the celebrated and much-beloved home of the Jews (Eretz Israel), with its capital, Jerusalem, presents a very sad spectacle to-day. All the glory of former days is vanished, and ruins mark the venerable magnificence of yore. Since the religious persecutions in Spain, Portugal and Italy, many Israelites settled in Palestine, consisting partly of those expelled from Spain, the so-called

Sefardim, or Portuguese, and partly also of Polish and German Jews, Ashkenazim, who form congregations and religious communities there.

Reminiscences of olden times, the holy love for the ancient land of promise, induced many Jews in all countries to emigrate to Palestine, where most of them subsist by the considerable sums of money sent there for their support by European and American co-religionists. These moneys are sent by almost every congregation to the Holy Land, and the proper authorities distribute them among beneficiaries in equitable proportion. This distribution is called *Chaluka*. Besides this, the European Jews are endeavoring to establish hospitals, schools, and many other charitable institutions. In recent years a strenuous effort is being made to counteract an evil, hitherto prevalent among the Palestinean Jews — the evil of indolence. Hitherto the only occupation of the Jews in Palestine was the study of the Talmud and Hebrew casuistry. Now they are forced to give their children proper education and instruction in profane science, and to qualify them either for agricultural or mechanical pursuits. Thanks also to the efforts of the Austrian Government, the social position of the Jews in Palestine has considerably improved, and while not yet on perfectly equal footing with their Christian and Mohammedan fellow-men, they approach steadily a state of full emancipation.

Several Jewish congregations exist also in Persia, Arabia and China, but we have very meager information of the same. In China, it is said, the Jews are perfectly free, enjoying the same rights as do the Chinese. Their language is a mixture of Hebrew and Persian. Their holy writings (as was mentioned above, Part II., Chap. i.) are divided into thirteen books, twelve of which are in honor of the twelve tribes, and one in honor of Moses. They observe the Sabbath and many other ceremonies, but do not understand the pure Hebrew language. The Jewish congregations in India, which stand under British dominion, consist of white and black Jews. The white Jews are engaged in commerce and agriculture, and enjoy many privileges which the black Jews are denied.

The black Jews descend from immigrants into India, married to black female slaves. They are rated much lower on the social scale, and are mostly mechanics. The colonists called Bene Israel, living at Bombay, Concan and other cities, are of Persian descent, and counted with the Indian Jews. This is a commercial tribe, leading a patriarchal life, and using the Indian language exclusively. They celebrate the Sabbath and the Day of Atonement.

VIII.—THE JEWS IN AFRICA.

With very few exceptions, the Jews of this continent, numbering one and a half million, are sorely oppressed. They occupy a very low position socially, especially in Morocco, Tunis and Tripoli, where they formerly enjoyed some rights and liberties. They are now excluded from all recognition of their rights, and seek in their religion a substitute for the earthly joys denied them; yet they sink lower and lower in ignorance and apathy. (It deserves to be noted that in 1823 a Jew from Fez was appointed consul-general for all European courts.) The Jews in Egypt are not more favored than their brethren in other African provinces. They, too, stand very low socially; wealth does not exist among them, or, if it does, in very rare and exceptional cases; poverty is the rule, and this brings on many dangerous sicknesses, which claim numerous victims.

The Falashahs, another Jewish tribe of Africa, inhabit Abyssinia. They are said to have settled in Africa as early as the time of the destruction of the first temple by Nebuchadnezzar (586 B. C.) Some of the customs practiced by them to-day may be traced back to the Mosaic law. They are subject to the Abyssinian princes, and their principal occupations are those of brickmakers, locksmiths and blacksmiths. Modern scholars devote their attention to the investigation of this tribe, of which but little is as yet known.

The Jewish population of Algiers, consisting of natives and immigrants, principally from France, had likewise much to endure. In 1847 they were exposed to the most cruel treatment. Sword, famine and utter misery effectively performed the work of decimation among them. Under French rule, their condition has materially improved, although even to-day their oppression in the uncivilized parts of Africa is of frequent occurrence. The great Israelitish institutions, the Alliance in France and the Board of Delegates of American Israelites, which in 1878 became part and parcel of the Union of American Hebrew Congregations, afford them powerful aid and protection.

IX.—THE JEWS IN AUSTRALIA.

On this continent, several thousand of our co-religionists have found a home. They are in fair circumstances. The first Jewish settlement was in Sydney, where they erected a beautiful synagogue, which has become a place to which all Australian Jews hasten, from their distant settlements and scattered habitations, whenever the high festivals attune the Jewish hearts to fervent devotion and earnest meditation. Within the past few years, however, several other congregations have been founded, prominent among which is that at Melbourne. They have houses of prayer and instruction, which are conducted after the model of European or American congregations.

X.—THE JEWS IN AMERICA.

When, in the fifteenth century, the fate of the Jews in Europe, and especially in Spain, was most deplorable, it was, as though by Divine Providence, that the New World was discovered, a country destined to become great and powerful, wealthy and influential, but above all the true and safe asylum for all oppressed people.

That noble mission of befriending the friendless, of sheltering the homeless, and granting true recognition to man by the standard of his merits only, America has most perfectly executed. Ever since the memorable Declaration of Independence, containing those assurances of securing to every man his inalienable rights of life, liberty and the pursuit of happiness, there has been perfect equality of all religions before the law. Nowhere has the constitution and the statute book been so true an exponent of the practice. The character and ability of a man are alone the tests of his worth, and not his descent or creed.

Jewish congregations are, therefore, the peers of all other congregations, and are fully recognized and protected by the law. In the United States of North America, and especially in the cities of New York, Chicago, Philadelphia, Cincinnati, Baltimore, Charleston, Savannah, Providence, New Orleans, San Francisco, etc., there are numerous congregations, governed by excellent laws and constitutions. Their temples are ornamental buildings, adorning the finest thoroughfares. Their grand institutions of charity and instruction are evidences not only of the wealth the Jews have acquired in this country, but of the charitable feelings hereditary in them as well.

The first Jewish settlers on American soil came from Spain at the time of the Inquisition. In 1624 they settled in Brazil, whence they went to Cayenne, where they found about 6,000 co-religionists, emigrants from Holland. When the French, in later years, destroyed this colony, the Jews went to Surinam, an English settlement, where they obtained perfect civil liberty, which they retained. In the seventeenth century they went to Central America, where they formed congregations. The greatest influx of European Jews to this great and blessed continent occurred since the beginning of this century.

The first Jewish settlement in the United States was in Newport, R. I., where they built a beautiful synagogue, acquired a fine cemetery, and established many other useful institutions. But Newport becoming too narrow for the development of Jewish talent and energy, they went to New York, the commercial metropolis of the New World. The synagogue at Newport is now empty, there being no Jewish congregation, yet it is kept in good repair through a legacy of Judah Touro, who was born there, and who, acquiring great wealth, most liberally endowed many charitable institutions, notably the " Touro Infirmary," at New Orleans, La. The oldest congregations were established in New York, Philadelphia, Savannah and Charleston, where the Portuguese prevailed. Since 1835 the influx of Jews into the United States from all parts of Europe has steadily increased, and the number of Jews now residing under the " stars and stripes " is over 250,000. In almost every city and town there now exists at least one Jewish congregation, and many own costly and magnificent buildings consecrated to the service of God.

In the city of New York, with her Jewish population of about 70,000, there are no less than twenty-nine synagogues; in Philadelphia, six; in Boston, three; in Charleston, two; in Richmond, two; in Savannah, one; in New Orleans, three; in Mobile, one; in Louisville, two; in Cincinnati, five; in St. Louis, three; in Chicago, five; in Detroit, two;

in Milwaukee, two; in San Francisco, four; in Cleveland, two; in Montgomery, one; in Atlanta, one; in Brooklyn and Williamsburg, three; etc.

In all, there are no less than 278 Hebrew congregations in the United States. Commercially the Jews in this Republic are very successful and financially prosperous, while many hold public office, municipal, legislative, judicial, etc. The schools and charitable institutions are highly creditable to them, and they enjoy the respect and esteem of their Christian fellow-citizens, as men, as merchants and as citizens.

XI.—THE GREAT JEWISH SOCIETIES.

The present century has witnessed the formation and establishment of many influential societies, called into existence by earnest, zealous Israelites, who aimed at the improvement of the condition of their brethren in countries where they yet suffer from the injustice, ignorance or ill-will of the masses. These institutions are to serve a three-fold purpose: (1) to support the unfortunate Jews by effective material assistance; (2) to further their spiritual development; and (3) to intercede in their behalf at those seats of government which are occupied by enlightened rulers, and from them to secure for their brethren humane treatment and justice.

Among these societies we must mention prominently the "Alliance Israelite Universelle," founded in France. The seat of this Alliance is Paris; the first President of the same was the late M. Adolphe Cremieux, once Minister of Justice of France. Up to his death (February, 1880) that great and eminent man presided at the deliberations of that body, and worked successfully in furtherance of the high object of that society. But though its seat is in Paris, its members and representatives are to be found throughout all civilized lands. It is owing to the laudable efforts of the "Alliance" that the Jews of the Orient — Africa, Turkey, Bulgaria, Roumania and other countries — are permitted to live as human beings, and to find protection against oppression. The "Alliance" has established and now maintains several religious, mechanical and industrial schools. The agricultural school at Joppa, established by the late Albert Cohn, of Paris, owes its existence, perpetuity and usefulness to the "Alliance."

Other similar societies are: The "Israelitish Alliance," of Vienna; the "Anglo-Jewish Association," at London; the "Shomer-Israel Society," in Lemberg, Galicia; and, last but by no means least, the influential "Board of Delegates of American Israelites" (since 1878 merged into the Union of American Hebrew Congregations—see below), which body has often and successfully pleaded the cause of the unfortunate Jews on other continents, before the government of this great Republic.

The original "Board of Delegates of American Israelites" was instituted about twenty years. It was established shortly after the abduction of Edgar Mortara. In order to carry out its designs more fully, and to extend its sphere of usefulness, it amalgamated with the "Union of American Hebrew Congregations," and is now known by the name of "Board of Delegates of Civil and Religious Rights," appointed by the Executive Board of the Union of American Hebrew Congregations, and has its seat in New York City.

In Leipsic, Germany, Mr. Maurice Kohner established, in 1869, "Der Deutsch Israelitische Gemeindebund" (Union of German Israelitish Congregations), whose object it is to guard the interests of the Congregations and their various institutions. Mr. Jacob Nachod is at present at the helm of this society, and the results achieved by it are quite encouraging.

Numerous "Teachers' Associations" are the product of recent years, and their object is the improvement of religious instruction and the support of indigent or disabled teachers, their widows and orphans. "Achava-Brotherhood" is the name of a most extensive and beneficial society; its seat is at Frankfort-on-the-Main.

In America there are, besides the "Union of American Hebrew Congregations," numerous other societies, such as the Orders "B'nai Berith," "Kesher Shel Barzel," "Free Sons of Israel," relief, charitable and benevolent societies, and various homes, hospitals and orphan asylums.

The Union of American Hebrew Congregations, established at Cincinnati in 1873, has for its object the establishment of a "Hebrew Theological College," the unification of American Jews, and the progress of Judaism. The Union is presided over by Mr. M. Loth, of Cincinnati, a gentleman well known throughout the country as a patriotic American, faithful Israelite, successful merchant, charitable man and author of several well-written and instructive novels, etc. The Chairman of the Executive Board is Mr. B. Bettmann, a gentleman quite and justly popular in Cincinnati. The number of Congregations constituting the membership of the Union amounts now to over 121, with a fair prospect of being further increased before long. It is universally conceded that American Judaism is considerably strengthened by this Union, which bids fair to fully accomplish the high object of its mission.

The objects of the Orders, or secret societies, in the United States, are the moral, social and intellectual advancement of Israelites, pecuniary benefit to members in case of sickness, and in case of death an endowment of $1,000 to $2,000 to their families. The Order B'nai Berith has seven Grand Lodges, with 327 Lodges and nearly 25,000 members.

The Order Kesher Shel Barzel has five Grand Lodges, 170 subordinate Lodges and 10,000 members.

The Order of Free Sons of Israel and Improved Order of Free Sons of Israel have three Grand Lodges, 130 subordinate Lodges and nearly 12,000 members.

The following hospitals belong to the Jews in the United States:

Mount Sinai Hospital, in New York.
Jewish Hospital, in Philadelphia.
Hebrew Hospital, in Baltimore.
Jewish Hospital, in Cincinnati.
Touro Infirmary, in New Orleans.

The orphan asylums and homes belonging to them are as follows:

Hebrew Benevolent and Orphan Asylum, in New York.
Foster Home and Orphan Asylum, in Philadelphia.
B'nai Berith Orphan Asylum, in Cleveland.
Jewish Orphan Asylum, in Baltimore.
Pacific Orphan Asylum, in San Francisco.
Home for Aged and Infirm, in Philadelphia.
Home for Aged and Infirm Hebrews, in New York.
Home for Widows and Orphans, in New Orleans.
Familien Waisen Verein, in Philadelphia.
Deborah Nursery and Child's Protectory, in New York.
Sheltering Guardian Society, in New York.

Other relief and charitable, free burial, fuel and free school societies, exist in almost every city.

The Jewish newspapers, magazines and periodicals published in the United States are:

Jewish Messenger, Hebrew Leader, Juedischer Gazetten, American Hebrew and *Jewish Advocate,* in New York.

Jewish Record, in Philadelphia.

Jewish South, in New Orleans.

American Israelite, Die Deborah, Sabbath Visitor, and *Hebrew* (quarterly) *Review*, in Cincinnati.

Jewish Tribune, in St. Louis.

Hebrew Observer, Hebrew, Times and *Progress*, in San Francisco.

Jewish Advance and *Occident*, in Chicago.

Zeitgeist, in Milwaukee.

XII.—RELIGIOUS TENDENCIES.

In the fundamental and cardinal doctrines of Judaism all Israelites agree. The sublime doctrine of the unity of God, expressed in the words, "Sh'ma Jisroel, Adonay Elohenu, Adonay Echod" (Hear, O Israel, the Eternal God is one in Unity), is regarded by all Israelites as the principal article of their faith. There are, consequently, no sects (in the general acceptation of the term) to be found among the professors of Judaism; yet there is among them a well-defined difference of view and of tendency. According to these differences, we distinguish in the ranks of Israelites, those of Orthodox, those of Reformed, and those of Conservative tendencies.

1. Orthodoxy — Rests upon the basis of Tradition and Schulchan Aruch. Orthodox, or strictly pious Jews, are very scrupulous in the observance of ceremonies and customs, and regard as criminal any deviation therefrom, however old and impracticable the forms may be. The dietary laws established by the rabbins are strictly observed by them. Not only do they abstain from the use of such food as is forbidden in the Pentateuch, but they also guard against a contamination of dishes used for cooking meats with those used for boiling milk, etc. Numerous ceremonies are observed at the birth, marriage or death of a person. The mode of worship they do not suffer to undergo the least change, and they

exclude from the synagogue, as irreligious, music and choral songs. Orthodoxy is losing ground from year to year. In America there is but very little, if any of it to be found. In Europe, however, Orthodoxy has yet some very stanch advocates and supporters.

2. Reform — Regards Judaism as capable of and destined for development. Its aim is to consider the requirements of the times, and to bring Judaism in accord with those claims, without, however, surrendering any essential and principal factors of Judaism. Reform seeks to abolish obsolete customs, to remodel forms and observances in accordance with reason, to introduce innovations on the basis of the essence of Judaism, as, for instance, the abbreviation of divine services, in order to secure more devotion; the omission of some prayers, which, by the change of circumstances, have become meaningless; the recitation of certain prayers in the vernacular, in order to impress those unacquainted with the Hebrew language; the introduction of the triennial cycle, *i. e.*, reading the Tora in three years, instead of completing it in one year, in order to afford the teachers of the congregations an opportunity to better and more thoroughly expound Scripture; the introduction of organ music to accompany the singing, as best calculated to enhance the devotion and edification of the worshipers. All these changes or reforms have received the sanction of synods, which, since 1846, have been held in Frankfort, Breslau, Leipsic, and other cities in Germany. In the United States, too, there have been held several conventions within the last twelve or fifteen years, for the purpose of establishing Reformed Judaism, which predominates here, and is now resting upon a solid foundation. There were rabbinical conferences held at Philadelphia, Cincinnati, Cleveland and New York, which, however, have been unsuccessful as yet in uniting all rabbis and congregations upon one common platform.

The question whether a synod should be convened or not is now agitating the minds of many representative American Jews.

3. Conservatism — Seeks to reconcile the differences of opinion, to harmonize the written law (Torah) and the oral law (Tradition) with the claims of this advanced age; to maintain venerable institutions, although purified and rendered more attractive, and to impart more sanctity and devotion to the divine service, not by discarding the traditional mode entirely, but by retaining it in the main, and only removing those features that are antagonistic to its purpose.

Among the most prominent representatives of Orthodoxy, we may mention the Rabbis Hirsh, Hildesheimer, Stern, Sofer, Spitzer, Lehman, Leeser, Morais and many Talmudists.

Of the champions of Reform, we mention Holdheim, Geiger, Loew, Phillippson, Szanto, Fassel, Jellinek, etc., in Europe; and Wise, Lilienthal, Einhorn, Hirsh, Adler, Gottheil, etc., in America.

Those of Conservative tendencies are Graetz, Frankl, Joel, Guedeman, Rahmer, Landau, etc., in Europe, and Huebsch, Jastrow, etc., in America.

The different tendencies are advocated not only from the pulpit, but more especially by the press, each of the three divisions having weekly or monthly periodicals. The organs of Orthodoxy are the *Israelit*, published by Lehman, in Mayence; *Jewish Press*, published by Meyer, in Berlin, and, during the lifetime of Leeser, the *Occident*, published by him in Philadelphia.

In the service of *Reform* there are the well-known and long-established *Allgemeine Zeitung des Judenthums*, published by Phillippson, in Bonn; *Neuzeit*, published by Szanto, in Vienna; **American Israelite**, edited by Wise, in

Cincinnati; *Zeitgeist*, published in Milwaukee; *Jewish Advance*, in Chicago, etc.

Conservatism is advocated by *Israelitische Wochenschrift*, by Rahmer, in Magdeburg; *Monatschrift*, a monthly periodical, formerly by Frankl and Graetz, now by the latter only, in Breslau; *Jewish Messenger*, by Isaacs, in New York, and many others.

XIII.—JEWISH INSTITUTIONS OF LEARNING.

With the improvement of the outward condition of the Israelites, their internal, or, rather, spiritual development has steadily kept pace. To improve mentally, to assist the needy and to fulfill their high calling was and is their aim, as the establishment and maintenance of grand institutions in most modern times amply testify.

Besides the magnificent places of devotion that have been erected in Europe and America and dedicated to the service of the ever-living God, there are schools, which enjoy the care and solicitude of all congregations. Of the numerous schools of importance in Germany, whose aim is the dissemination of the seeds of religious knowledge and science among the young, we mention prominently:

1. The Franz School, in Dessau, the birthplace of Mendelssohn, at which men of great ability were active.

2. Jacobsohn's School, in Seesen, established by Israel Jacobsohn (1768–1828), one of the most prominent men of German Israel, who endowed that institution with $100,000. This school affords instruction not only to indigent students, for whose benefit the generous founder at first intended it, but even many wealthy and non-Jewish parents intrust their children to this seat of learning, where good education and thorough instruction are to be obtained.

3. The Samson School, at Wolfenbuettel, similar in plan and tendency to the Jacobsohn School.

In addition to these and other similar schools, to be found in almost every large city of Germany, Austria and Hungary, whose object it is to spread the knowledge of profane and sacred literature, there are now also high-schools, founded for the purpose of training teachers and rabbis. The various seminaries furnish Jewish congregations with capable teachers, ministers, cantors, etc. In former times there were only numerous "Yeshiboth," that is, academies of Talmud, in which rabbinical authorities taught Theological discipline. Many of those Yeshiboth exist to this day, as, for instance, the Yeshiba, in Preszburg, Hungary, attended by 400 Talmud students (Bachurim), and the many similar places of learning in Russia, Poland, etc. But these institutions fail to satisfy the claims of a progressive age, affording only a one-sided education, while it is expected that the religious guide of a congregation should not only possess a thorough knowledge of the Talmud, but likewise be fully conversant with the entire Hebrew and kindred literature, with philosophy and the classics, in order that they might be the true representatives of Judaism, not only religiously, but also scientifically. To this purpose public rabbinical schools or theological colleges were founded, of which the following are to be noticed:

1. The Rabbinical Seminary at Breslau, founded about 1855, which, during the quarter of a century of its existence, has accomplished much good for Judaism. Great men of science, scholars of world-wide celebrity, have been and are now active there; thus, the President, Zacharias Frankl (lately deceased), Professors Graetz, Lazarus and others. Many rabbis, now filling pulpits in Germany and here in the United States, are graduates of that seminary. The tendency of this justly celebrated institution is Conservative, maintaining the traditional standpoint of Judaism, and

seeking to reconcile it with the results of scientific researches.

2. The High-School for the Knowledge of Judaism at Berlin, with Reformed tendency, was founded and for some time conducted by the celebrated rabbi and author, the late Dr. Abraham Geiger (died in 1874).

3. The Theological Institute or "the great Beth Ham-Midrash," at Vienna, called into existence and presided over by the well-known scholar and celebrated preacher, the Rev. Dr. Adolph Jellinek. He is ably assisted by the erudite Talmudists and profound exegetists, the Lectors J. H. Weisz, M. Friedman and others. The object of this Institute is to spread thorough and varied knowledge. It is perfectly neutral with regard to religious tendency, leaving it optional with the student to adopt either Reformed, Orthodox or Conservative views.

4. The Rabbinical Seminary for Orthodox Judaism in Berlin. Dr. Hildesheimer, one of the prominent representatives of Orthodoxy, who formerly resided at Eisenstedt, Hungary, and there founded and presided over an Orthodox rabbinical school, transferred it to Berlin, on his removal to the German capital, and now directs it there, under the name given above.

5. The Hungarian Rabbinical School at Buda-Pest, Hungary, recently established, resembles, in its polity, organization and tendency, the seminary in Breslau.

Similar other institutions are to be found in a more or less flourishing condition, at Metz, Lemberg, Cincinnati and other cities. The Cincinnati Hebrew Union College we shall notice more at length below.

In the United States of America there are schools for religious instruction connected with almost every congregation. In these schools, generally superintended by the rabbi, minister or teacher, children from the age of six or seven to that of thirteen or fourteen are instructed in Hebrew, Biblical History and Catechism. The sessions of these schools are held mostly on Sundays (the other days of the week being devoted to secular instruction), hence their name of Sunday-schools.

The rite of confirmation, conferred upon children of proper age and sufficient information, generally closes their religious instruction, after which it is supposed that by attending the regular divine services at the house of worship and listening to the religious discourses of the ministers, they increase their knowledge of and become strengthened in their adherence to Judaism.

In large cities, where poor Israelites reside, their children enjoy the benefits of religious instruction in regularly-established and well-endowed Hebrew free schools.

Both in Europe and in this country there has been a long-felt want for rabbis properly trained and thoroughly familiar with classical and Hebrew lore. The graduates of European seminaries heretofore called to fill pulpits on this continent fail more and more to satisfy the claims of American congregations, in proportion as these congregations lose their foreign character. This failure of the European seminarists is not owing to any lack of thoroughness or information, but partly to their ignorance of the English language and partly to the want of a proper appreciation of American conditions. An American theological college was what was needed. In 1855 an attempt was made in Cincinnati to establish the Zion College; and in 1858 an attempt was made at Philadelphia, and the Maimonides College was founded; but, owing to several causes, they were short-lived, and ere they had an opportunity to produce proofs of their vital power they ceased to exist. To the perseverance and unremitting efforts of the zealous and indefatigable worker for the cause of Judaism in America, the

Rev. Dr. I. M. Wise, it is mainly due that such a college is at last firmly established, founded on a solid basis, and bidding fair to accomplish much good for American Judaism.

As mentioned above (Part III., Chap. xi.), a Union of American Hebrew Congregations was effected at Cincinnati, in 1873. The avowed object of this Union was the establishment of a theological college. In September, 1875, a preparatory class was opened. The Rev. Dr. I. M. Wise was appointed President, and the Rev. Dr. M. Lilienthal Professor of the embryo college. Every succeeding year a new class was added, until the summer of 1879 witnessed the completion of the preparatory course. In the fall of the same year the college proper was opened, with the graduates of the preparatory schools at Cincinnati and New York. The collegiate course is calculated to consume four years, after a four years' preparatory course, so that after eight years' training and study of Hebrew literature and science in all their branches, the student (who, on entering the Hebrew Union College, must be either an attendant at or a graduate of a high-school or university) becomes qualified as rabbi.

Up to May, 1881, the instruction to the students was imparted in the school-rooms of the two principal congregations (Dr. Wise's and Dr. Lilienthal's) alternately. On April 24th a most magnificent and commodious building, which had been purchased and fitted up for the purpose, was dedicated and opened as the Hebrew Union College. The Rev Dr. I. M. Wise is the President, and teaches Philosophy; the Rev. Dr. M. Lilienthal is Professor of History; the Rev. Dr. M. Mielziner, Professor of Talmud, etc. The Faculty comprises also two Preceptors, the Messrs. Aufrecht and Eppinger.

A very valuable library of some 8,000 volumes is connected with and owned by the college. A preparatory school of the Cincinnati college exists also in New York, superintended by that learned and zealous champion of Judaism, the Rev. Dr G. Gottheil, who is ably assisted by an efficient staff of teachers. These schools at New York and Cincinnati are maintained by the Union of American Hebrew Congregations, who annually appoint a commission, composed of learned and disinterested gentlemen, to examine into the management of the schools, and the efficiency and progress of the students.

XIV.—ISRAELITISH CELEBRITIES.

In every walk of public life we now find Israel's great men active. What the immortal Moses Mendelssohn sought and strove for was continued and furthered by public-spirited and enlightened men, and these, no less than their illustrious prototype, deserve all Israel's everlasting gratitude, reverence and admiration. Among these celebrities we find savants, rabbis, authors, thinkers and poets.

Sachs, Zunz, Rappaport, Beer, Phillippson, Luzzato, Frankl, Herxheimer, Geiger, Munk, Jellinek, Einhorn, Fuerst, Dukes, Neubauer, Cassel, Steinschneider, Goldschmidt, Jost, Graetz, Herzfeld, Adler, Kaempf, Joel, Kayserling, Rahmer, Auerbach, Guedeman, Wise, Lilienthal, Gottheil, Jastrow, Huebsch, Hirsch, Kohlêr and many more in this as on the transatlantic continent, are men who have secured for themselves a niche in the Temple of Fame, men upon whom Israel may look with just pride.

Among the great men of modern times we also find such eminent Talmudists as Moses Sofer, Akiba Eger, Jonathan Eibenschuetz, Bineth Muentz, Frankl, Weisz, Friedman and others.

To the most prominent pulpit orators of the present age belong men like Sachs, Solomon, Holdheim, Mannheimer, Meisel, Jellinek, Philippson, Goldschmidt, Stein, Einhorn,

Leeser, Raphall, Huebsch, Sonneschein, Kohler, Hirsch, Gottheil and others.

Eminent historiographers are Jost, Graetz, Kayserling, E. Hecht, Salvator, Wolf, Wise, Raphall, etc.

Philosophers, Schmiedl, Joel and others.

We have also great exegetists, eminent philologists and acknowledged *literati* in great number.

To the most celebrated singers of synagogical music (Chazanim) belong, first and foremost, Sulzer; next, Levandowsky, Naumburg, Weintraub, Friedman, Goldstein, Katschmaroff, Rubin, etc.

Besides those Israelites who devote their lives to Judaism and its science, we find others celebrated as philosophers, physicians, jurists, astronomers, poets, artists, statesmen, etc.

Lazarus, Steinthal, Traube, Cremieux, Rieser, Lasker, Kuranda, Levy, Auerbach, L. A. Frankl, Kompert, Mosenthal, Kaulbach, Oppenheim, Madame Rachel, Sonnenthal, Rott, Meyerbeer, Halevi, Goldmark, Ezekiel, Noah, Judah P. Benjamin, Simon Wolf, B. F. Peixotto, Ellinger, Joachimsen and others too numerous to mention, are names which are universally admired and honored.

And who could mention all the great men in Israel who did or do excel as merchants, artists, artisans, scientists, etc.?

But before we close this chapter of celebrities in Israel we must mention some who, as the benefactors of their race, have immortalized their names—who have founded or endowed homes for the poor, the aged or infirm, hospitals for the sick, asylums for the fatherless, for the blind, the deaf and the mute, or schools for the ignorant.

There is, first and foremost, that pride of Israel, the hoary-headed, patriarchal, generous and illustrious Sir Moses Montefiore (whom may God grant yet many years of life, health and usefulness 1); the Rothschilds in England, Austria and Germany; Hirsch, Goldsmith, Koenigswarter, Wertheim, etc., in Austria, and, above all, the host of men and noble women in this country whose praises are best and most worthily proclaimed by those grand institutions of charity, supported and maintained by the wealth wherewith **God has** blessed them.

XV.—STATISTICS.

The number of Israelites throughout the earth is variously estimated as low as 7,500,000 and as high as 10,000,000 (Christians at between 400,000,000 and 500,000,000, Mohammedans at between 170,000,000 and 200,000,000, and Heathens at between 850,000,000 and 900,000,000).

Of these 7,000,000 or more of Israelites, there are in Europe 5,000,000 to 5,500,000; in Asia, 750,000 to 1,000,000; in Africa, 500,000 to 750,000; in North America, 230,000 to 280,000, and some in Australia.

The European States have a Jewish population approximating the following numbers:

1. Poland	1,000,000	10. Switzerland	10,000
2. Austro-Hungary	1,500,000	11. Servia	2,000
3. Roumania	200,000	12. France	48,000
4. Russia (nearly)	2,000,000	13. Great Britain	48,000
5. Netherlands	70,000	14. Italy	36,000
6. Germany	511,000	15. Norway	2,000
7. Turkey	100,000	16. Sweden	2,000
8. Greece	5,000	17. Belgium	2,000
9. Denmark	5,000	18. Spain-Portugal	7,000

Arranged according to the three great national families, we find that by far the greatest number of European Israelites (over 5,000,000) live among the people of Slavonian tongue; the Romanic countries have only about 100,000, and **the** Germanic about 850,000.

Most of the Israelites in Germany live in Posen, Bromberg, Wiesbaden, Marienwerder, Cassel, Unterfranken, Berlin, Breslau, Hamburg, Altona, Stettin, Frankfort-on-the-Main, Mannheim, Strasburg, Muehlhausen, Leipsic, Dresden, Munich, Fuerth and Mayence.

The largest Jewish Congregations in Europe are in Buda-Pest, Vienna, Cracow, Lemberg, London, Prague, Warsaw, St. Petersburg, Brody, Bucharest, Paris, and Constantinople.

In America, most of the Jews live in the following States: New York, Pennsylvania, Maryland, Ohio, California, Illinois, Kentucky and Louisiana.

The largest congregations in the United States are the following: In New York City, Temple Emanu-El, Ahavath Chesed, Beth-El and Sherith Israel; in Philadelphia, Rodef Sholem, Mikve Israel, Keneseth Israel, etc.; in Cincinnati, B'nai Israel and B'nai Yeshurun; in Baltimore, Har Sinai and Oheb Sholem; in Chicago, Sinai, Zion and Anshe Maariv; in Louisville, Adath Israel; in New Orleans, Sinai and Gates of Prayer; in St. Louis, Shaare Emeth and B'nai-El; in San Francisco, Emanu-El and Ohabai Sholom; in Savannah, Mikve Israel; in New Haven, Mishkan Israel.

From the statistical tables published by order of the Union of American Hebrew Congregations in 1880, whence the above and other data are taken, it is seen that there are in all 278 congregations in the United States, with an aggregate membership of about 13,000. The Sabbath-schools connected with the various congregations are attended by nearly 13,500 children, while the value of real estate and other property owned by them is calculated at about $7,000,000.

CONCLUSION.

OUR DUTY IN THE PRESENT AND FOR THE FUTURE.

We have thus as briefly as possible sketched the history of our people; a history so rich in thrilling incidents, so fraught with valuable lessons, so inspiring and comforting! This wonderful record of this remarkable people, whose sublime mission and high destiny no one can deny, is in itself a faithful guide and instructor. It clearly points out the ways of Providence, and marks the goal for which we are to strive. It is a true index of the progress of time, of the improvement of the world and its inhabitants. For no people on earth, among the many whose road was a thorny one, has suffered as much as Israel; none was more persecuted or oppressed for its religious views than were the Jews. And, though their faith was the mother of all monotheistic religions, yet the children have proven wayward and rebellious. But this indescribable suffering of Israel is at the same time evidence, unmistakable and undeniable, of an all-kind Providence, watching over and guarding the fate of its first-born son. Israel's history represents in its entirety a battle for existence, lasting thousands of years, a battle in which the divine grace was revealed to the struggling sons of Jacob. All the nations of gray antiquity have fallen and passed away; the ancient people of the covenant of God—Israel alone—has withstood all the terrible attacks from without, because it bears within the germ of indestructibility. That people, which was destined to become the priest-people and a holy nation—*i. e.*, not a powerful nation, in possession of an extensive territorial domain, but only a people, the receptacle of true religion, the maintainer and disseminator of the purest and most sublime idea concerning God, virtue and morality — that people can not, will never perish. More than 1800 years ago it started on its world-redeeming mission. Through night and darkness, through fire and water, along the verge of dangerous abysses, past crumbling worlds and decaying institutions, lay its way; but gradually the mists of that dreary darkness were dispelled by the potent agency of Israel's torch of light and truth. Step by step the Jews have victoriously advanced; the intellectual world recognizes their influence for good, and freely admits that many blessings enjoyed in these days and many improvements that mark the present era are directly the result of Israel's faith.

It is true that even now specters rise from the darkness of their mediæval tombs, that even in this age they now and then raise their heads and disclose their horribly contorted features in the light of the sun of civilization; it is true that prejudices, hatred, malice and envy still tend to imbitter the fate of this often and sorely-tried people; it is true that even in Germany, the seat of modern learning and thought, an Anti-Semitic agitation has been set on foot within the last few years; that divines, historians and scholars not only favor, but strongly advocate, a measure which tends to deprive the Israelites of their full rights as German citizens; it is true that indescribable woe has within this year (1881) befallen the Jews of Southern Russia; — but all these signs, painful as they certainly are, and trying to the patience of our brethren as they necessarily must be, are but the last agonies, the convulsions preceding the total dissolution of the monster.

Out of the 40,000,000 and more inhabitants of Germany who were expected or requested by the leaders of the Anti·

Semitic League to sign a petition to the government for the abrogation of the rights of the Jews, there were less than one-half per cent. of that number base enough to sanction so degrading a scheme.

The greatest men in Germany, excelling in art, science or statesmanship, such as Professors Virchow, Mommsen and others, leaders of the German Parliament, and, above all, the hope and joy of the Germans, the noble-hearted and illustrious Crown Prince, unqualifiedly condemn those men of narrow minds and their measures.

In Russia the government has taken energetic steps to protect the Jews exposed to the fury of the mob, and to bring to condign punishment the offenders.

In Spain, the country of Torquemada and the Inquisition, time has brought about a most gratifying change. Desirous of atoning for the Inquisition of Ferdinand and Isabella, his predecessors on the Spanish throne, King Alphonso, hearing of the inhuman treatment, persecution and banishment to which the Russian Jews are exposed at present, has extended to them a most cordial invitation to settle again in the land their fathers had loved so well.

And, therefore, while we have reason to look hopefully into the future, we may by no means consider our work completed, our mission ended.

To strengthen our cause, and with it the cause of humanity, we should ever keep before our mind the valuable lessons taught by the history of Israel. The noble examples of those that have gone before us must urge us on to emulate them; and truth and light and knowledge must be spread until they have become common property. Peace and harmony must prevail and the covenant which God made with our forefathers, and which they have bequeathed to us, we must in our turn renew and bequeath to our posterity. The reconciliation of all discordant elements, the fraternization of all mankind, is the goal which we should with all our power strive to reach.

[THE END.]

CHRONOLOGICAL TABLE.*

	B. C.
The Biblical Annals close, about.	400
Alexander the Great conquers Palestine.	332
The Jews under the rule of the Egyptian Ptolemies	323— 221
The Jews under Syrian rule.	221
Antiochus Epiphanes becomes King.	175
The War for Independence begins under Matthias.	167
Juda Maccabi	166— 160
Jonathan	160— 143
Simon rules as Prince.	143— 135
John Hyrcanos.	135— 106
Herod's reign begins.	37

	C. E.
Herod's reign ends.	3
Hillel and Shammai, Sanhedrial Chiefs	91
Roman Procurators appointed.	7
" continued till.	37
" appointed again.	44— 70
Destruction of Jerusalem and the Temple	70
Bar Cochba	130
Fall of Bethar—Akiba's death.	135
Simon ben Gamaliel	180
Period of Amoraïm begins with Jehudah Hanassi, the compiler of the Mishna.	170
Mishna completed.	210
The Jerusalem Talmud published, about.	370
Rab Ashe publishes the Babylonian Talmud.	400
Rabina completes it, about.	500
Sabureans	500— 550
Gaonim	589—1038
Bulan, King of the Chazares, becomes a Jew	731
Anan founds the sect of Caraites	754
Saadja.	892— 942

* After M. Elkan.

Solomon Ibn Gabirol	1020—1070
Rashi	1040—1105
The Crusades	1096
Ibn Ezra	1088—1167
Alphes dies	1103
Maimonides (Rambam)	1135—1204
Jehudah Halevi dies	1150
Nachmanides (Ramban)	1194—1268
The Jews banished from England	1290
Maharam (Meyer ben Baruch) dies	1293
Persecution of the Jews in Spain	1391
The Jews banished from Spain	1492
Don Isaac Abarbanel	1492
Sabbathai Zevi	1626—1676
Manasse ben Israel—Spinoza—Return of the Jews to England	1655
Moses Mendelssohn	1729—1786
First Rabbinical Conference	1844
Second " "	1845
Third " "	1846
Dedication of the Breslau Seminary	1854
Union of American Hebrew Congregations founded	1873
Dedication of the Hebrew Union College	1881

CPSIA information can be obtained
at www.ICGtesting.com
Printed in the USA
BVHW090103211118
533638BV00011B/549/P